THE MYSTIC LIFE

TEACHINGS OF
THE ORDER OF CHRISTIAN MYSTICS

THE MYSTIC LIFE

TEACHINGS OF THE ORDER OF CHRISTIAN MYSTICS

THE "CURTISS BOOKS" FREELY AVAILABLE AT

WWW.ORDEROFCHRISTIANMYSTICS.CO.ZA

1. THE VOICE OF ISIS
2. THE MESSAGE OF AQUARIA
3. THE INNER RADIANCE
4. REALMS OF THE LIVING DEAD
5. COMING WORLD CHANGES
6. THE KEY TO THE UNIVERSE
7. THE KEY OF DESTINY
8. LETTERS FROM THE TEACHER VOLUME I
9. LETTERS FROM THE TEACHER VOLUME II
10. THE TRUTH ABOUT EVOLUTION AND THE BIBLE
11. THE PHILOSOPHY OF WAR
12. PERSONAL SURVIVAL
13. THE PATTERN LIFE
14. FOUR-FOLD HEALTH
15. VITAMINS
16. WHY ARE WE HERE?
17. REINCARNATION
18. FOR YOUNG SOULS
19. GEMS OF MYSTICISM
20. THE TEMPLE OF SILENCE
21. THE DIVINE MOTHER
22. THE SOUNDLESS SOUND
23. THE MYSTIC LIFE
24. THE LOVE OF RABIACCA
25. POTENT PRAYERS

SUPPORTING VOLUMES

26. THE SEVENTH SEAL
27. TOWARDS THE LIGHT

THE MYSTIC LIFE

Transcribed by
HARRIETTE AUGUSTA CURTISS
and
F. HOMER CURTISS, B.S., M.D.
Founders of
THE ORDER OF CHRISTIAN MYSTICS
and
AUTHORS OF THE "CURTISS BOOKS"

2012 EDITION

REPUBLISHED FOR THE ORDER BY
MOUNT LINDEN PUBLISHING
JOHANNESBURG, SOUTH AFRICA
ISBN: 978-1-920483-21-0

Dedication

This edition is lovingly dedicated to the Memory

of the Founders of

The Order of Christian Mystics

Pyrahmos and Rahmea

and to

The Teacher of the Order

who on earth was called

Helena Petrovna Blavatsky

"Ministers of Christ and Stewards of the Mysteries of God."
1 Corinthians 4 vs. 1

COPYRIGHT 2012
BY

MOUNT LINDEN PUBLISHING

First Published in 1934

May be used for non-commercial, personal, research and educational use.
ALL RIGHTS RESERVED

CONTENTS

Preface	v
The mystic life	1
The path of discipleship	34
Illumination	52
The mystic Christ	66
Recommendations for daily life	92

Appendix
    Announcement of the Order 101
    The Fellowship of the Order of Christian Mystics . . . 102
    Organizations 108
    As to Other Movements 109
    Special Objects of the Order 117
    Financial Obligations 122
    The Object of Study Classes 127
    How to Form a Study Class 128
    Order of Service 133
    The Prayers of the Order 134
    Index 140

PREFACE

THE Teachings of *The Order of Christian Mystics* (also known as *The Order of the Fifteen*), of which the following pages form a part, have been issued privately to students each month continuously since 1908. In view of their great value to the spiritual growth of these students, who now comprise residents of over seventy different countries of the world, this booklet is issued so that the Teachings may be more widely introduced to the general public in popular form.

A description of the aims and objects of this non-sectarian, uplifting, unifying, spiritual movement will be found in the *Appendix* herein.

THE MYSTIC LIFE

CHAPTER I

How Christian Mysticism Solves the World Problems[1]

The life of causes.

THE Mystic Life is the life of causes, the life of realization, the life of the Soul, the manifestation of the inner through the outer. It is called mystical because it is a manifestation of a mystery; for all life is a mystery. All manifestation comes from the unseen. All the myriad forms we see around us in Nature appear from out the unseen, apparently self-generated. For there is no life, consciousness, nor creative and formative power in matter itself. Matter is only the substance with which un-

---

[1] An address delivered by F. Homer Curtiss, M. D., Co-founder of *The Order of Christian Mystics*, before the Second Parliament of Religions of the World Fellowship of Faiths at the Morrison Hotel in Chicago at 8 P.M., on September 13th, 1933.

seen forces and intelligences clothe themselves to manifest for a short cycle here on Earth. Therefore nothing that we see in the outer world around us is the thing itself. It is only a shell or instrument through which the mystic Life of Causation finds expression.

A mystic not a dreamer.

A mystic is one who is not satisfied with the study of the mere outer forms of manifestation, the mere physical vehicles and the various phenomena connected with their manifestation. A mystic is one who wants to get behind the seen into the unseen. He wants to go back of the outer phenomena of life and study their causes; for only so can he really understand their manifestation.

A true mystic, therefore, is not a mere dreamer. He is not one who spends his time in idle speculation. Still less is he one who thinks so vaguely that his mind is in a mental mist, a fog of impractical intellectual or metaphysical speculations. A true mystic is one who seeks the Real back of the seeming; the Reality back of all outer manifestations. He is one who seeks to penetrate the mists of radiant glory that forever surround the throne of the Creator, the true cause and source of all manifestation. And he tries to apply the realization of these basic truths to his daily life. For the mystic, therefore, the highest ideal of each phase of life is the only goal worthy of striving for.

Our many lives.

The mystic sees that we live many aspects of life within our one life. We have our outer life that we live before the world and whose achievements may be worthy for history to record as constituting our life. That is our outer, public or physical life. Then we have a life that is known only to our family and close friends. That is our personal life. Then we have our mental life which is shared only by those of like mind and ideas.

We also have our psychic life in which we commune with our loved ones who have finished their work here on earth and have withdrawn from the outer physical body to continue their life manifestation in a finer body, "One flight up with their overcoats off" as we express it.[2] We also have our own life in those higher realms when we withdraw from the physical during sleep and mingle with our loved ones up there in that higher school of life. For, remember, *there is no death*. Only a withdrawal from a temporary and lower manifestation of life to function in a higher.

The Real Life.

But back of all, we have that Inner Life of the Soul, that Real Self which is the Real Life and which animates all the forms in which we may manifest on all planes in all the worlds of manifestation. That is the mysterious Inner Self whose inner urge keeps us ever seeking, ever striving. Striving for what? For satisfaction. And why? That we may attain

---

[2] For details see *Realms of the Living Dead*, Curtiss.

that happiness whose ultimate is heavenly bliss; that "peace which passeth understanding"; the realization of the consciousness of the Divine within us.

The source of happiness.

Unfortunately the unfoldment of the vast majority of mankind enables them to live for the most part only in the consciousness of the outer world and to respond as a rule only to the vibrations which reach their consciousness through the five physical senses. Therefore they naturally seek satisfaction and happiness through these senses. They naturally seek it in things, in possessions, in outer attainments, in the gratification of the animal desires, appetites, and passions.

But no true satisfaction can be attained when the inner is made to vibrate only to the outer. There may be a certain degree of pleasurable sensations from without, but they culminate only in satiety, not true satisfaction or happiness. True satisfaction and happiness are attained only from within outward; only when the outer is made to vibrate to the inner; when manifestation responds to causation, the personality to the Inner Self or Soul.

Therefore the mystic solves the great basic problem of human happiness by *seeking it within* instead of without; by seeking that inner guidance from within which shall so order and direct the thoughts, the words and the deeds of the outer life that it shall give ever greater expression to that Divine Self within which is striving for expression, and thus attain that happiness which comes only when the Divine within has found at least some degree of manifestation in the world without.

Express love now.

Happiness is, therefore, not merely a transient and ephemeral vibration of the outer senses. It is a manifestation of an essential Soul quality. Hence, when we say or do something that makes others happy, we are awakening and bringing into expression a Soul vibration in them. And this vibration is expansive, creative, and constructive. For no vibration of inharmony, antagonism, evil, or sin can find expression when the whole being is expressing happiness.

And it takes so little to make people happy! A kind word or act; a nod and a pleasant smile; an unselfish deed. A flower or a postcard or other remembrance. A word of sympathy or of appreciation may brighten and make happy a whole day of depression or discouragement or of otherwise routine work. And the happiness returns every time one thinks of it. So do not wait to "say it with flowers" after a loved one is gone. Express your love, your appreciation or your approval here and now. Do not do it in such a way as to flatter or make them vain, but to express your appreciation of the good, the beautiful, and the true in others and encourage them in its expression.

The mystic lives life.

The true mystic is, therefore, the happiest person in the world, and he naturally radiates that vibration of peace, harmony, and the joy of living to all he contacts. For he has realized within himself the joy of living in harmony with the Divine within. And having found the source of true happiness within he naturally wants everyone else to be happy likewise.

Since he finds his happiness here and now, he does not have to wait until he goes to heaven to experience it. He is, therefore, not one who seeks to get away from life, but one who seeks to *live life* to its *fullest and highest*; to let the highest spiritual vibrations dominate and thrill the human personality and thus give it its greatest satisfaction and happiness. He seeks to perfect the animal body and develop the mind, not for their own sake, but only that they may become more perfect instruments for the expression of the indwelling Soul.

The Law of Manifestation.

But since the mystic has studied the Laws of Causation he has learned that the Law of Sacrifice underlies the Law of Manifestation. Therefore, he understands that to bring happiness to others he must give something of himself and thus become an integral part of an open channel for the fulfillment of at least a tiny expression of that great Cosmic Law of Sacrifice.

The Law of Sacrifice.

Through an understanding of this Law he realizes that on the downward arc of manifesting the Unmanifested—called the Cycle of Necessity—the Greater must sacrifice Itself that the lesser may manifest and have an individualized expression of the One Divine Life which animates all forms of life. For just as the physical Sun sacrifices its light, life, warmth, and radiant energy that all the seeds and germs and countless forms of life may sprout and grow and have their tiny individual expressions of life, so does God—the Creator and Manifestor of all—sacrifice His oneness that the multitudes may manifest.

The Seven Archangels.

Through this Law He sacrifices His Unity that Duality may spring forth.

And Duality sacrifices itself that the Trinity may find expression. And from the Trinity there is generated that sevenfold expression of the God-head which underlies the structure of all manifested life.[3] First we have "The seven Spirits which are before His throne. . . . the seven angels which stood before God. . . . the seven Spirits of God sent forth into all the earth," as the book of *Revelation* tells us. These are the seven mighty Archangels who are the Planetary Deities who rule the seven sacred planets of our solar system. From these great Angels there radiate the seven great Hierarchies of lesser Celestial Beings which bring into expression every ideal in the mind of God that is to make up the manifested universe.

Evolution begins.

And when the cycle of outgoing has been completed and the higher forms of

---

[3] The seven Creative Spirits, the Dhyan Chohans, who correspond to the Hebrew Elohim. For details see the chapters on number 7 in *The Key of the Universe*, Curtiss.

manifestation have each sacrificed some thing of themselves that lesser forms may manifest, and so on down until the mineral kingdom is reached, then the reverse process begins and the upward arc or the cycle of evolution starts.

The Cycle of Necessity.

The mineral sacrifices its form of life, or, we may say, is killed and eaten, that a higher form of the One Life, the vegetable, may find expression. The vegetable, in turn, sacrifices its form of life, is killed and eaten, that a higher form, the animal, may manifest. The animal, in turn, sacrifices its form of life that a still higher form of life, man, may live. And man, the animal self and the human personality, must sacrifice its life; that is, give up its selfishness, its self will, its vanities, ambitions, and desires, in such a complete surrender that it corresponds to being killed and eaten or swallowed up, and all its powers absorbed and utilized that the highest form of life, the Real or Spiritual Self, may find expression through it and thus complete the Cycle of Necessity by the union of the individualized Spirit with its Source.

In this way the sacrifice of each form to a higher form receives its compensation by being built into that form and experiencing and being uplifted by the vibrations of a higher form of life which is expressing vibrations of life which are many octaves above those of the lower form. It therefore follows that no form of life has a right to take the life of another form unless it can furnish it some corresponding compensation.

How God expresses in humanity.

Thus we see that just as God submitted Himself to this cosmic and universal Law of Sacrifice that we might have individualized expression, so must we submit to this same Law of Sacrifice by giving up our wills, our hearts, our lives that we may be swallowed up and absorbed in Him that He may find expression through us. For, remember, that *we mortals are the only avenues* or means *through which God can find expression in humanity!* We all know how necessary God is to us. But did you ever stop to think *how necessary we are to God?* It is a tremendous concept to realize that without our making ourselves holy channels for the expression of His Life, His love, His compassion, His blissful happiness, we are hampering His manifestation. Once we have realized this great concept, how glad and willing and how joyous should be our complete surrender to Him!

We must voluntarily choose.

This may seem very mystical and impractical at first sight, but it has a very practical application. For just as the light and life of the Sun is poured out to be embodied in the plants and all growing things, so is the Light and Life of the Spiritual Sun poured out to be embodied in us as spiritual enlightenment, which we call the Christ-consciousness or our spiritual guidance in all our affairs.

But just as the sunlight does the plant no good unless the plant absorbs it, so the light, life and love of God does us no good *unless we correlate with and absorb it*. The Sun cannot compel the plant to absorb its rays, neither can God compel us to absorb the down-pouring of His forces that we may grow spiritually. And still less can He make us sacrifice ourselves to and become absorbed in Him. Those are things that *we must voluntarily choose to do* because we desire to. This we do through meditation on Him, through prayer, aspiration, and constant devotion to Him.

This is not a matter of the brain, but of the heart. Therefore great education, great learning and a highly developed intellect are not necessary. Only a tender, loving heart; only a steadfast desire to know and be one with Him; only an open, receptive, child-like mind that is willing to be taught of God and is willing to obey Him. That is all that is necessary.

The one Source.

This law is of universal application. For since it requires no creed, no dogma, no ritual, it is applicable to all mankind, no matter what their stage of intellectual unfoldment, their religion, their creed, their color, or their race may be. For all mankind are emanations from one of the seven great Archangels, and it makes no difference what the color of the Ray of which they are a part. The Source of all the Rays is the same, the One Eternal Being who is above and beyond all human, finite conception, call Him by what name or term you will.

The Sun is the one central orb of light and life to our solar system, no matter by what name it is called in various languages. So the Spiritual Sun, the Sun of Righteousness, is the one central source of spiritual light, life, and love in the universe, no matter what name He is called or how He is worshipped in the various religions. The only thing that counts is, *is He recognized* in some way, *sought for and correlated with* through some form of worship, and *embodied and expressed* in our lives?

It therefore matters little what the form of the worship or ritual may be. All who worship God are necessarily worshipping the same God; for He is one God, not many, although He manifests under and through all the Divine Beings who compose His Hierarchies of Manifestation, just as the Sun manifests through the seven color rays of the rainbow.

Each religion a Path to God.

Once one's mind is trained from childhood to seek for and correlate with Him through one religion or one Path of Light, one should be devoted to that religion and walk up that Path to Him. One should follow the race-thought in which he was brought up. He should, therefore, not change his religion except under unusual circumstances, and then only as a result of his own Divine Guidance from within and not from argument or the emotional storm of a revival service. For each religion is a Path of Light leading to God if its highest ideals are grasped and followed and embodied in the life.

It is only the childish conceit of a very limited outlook on life that makes the followers of any one religion claim that it is the best and only true religion. All religions and forms of worship which lead their devotees to a *personal realization* and *ultimate union* with their ideal of God are true religions. On a moonlit lake the silver path to the Moon is seen a little differently from every boat on the lake. And it is only by following the path that shines down to our boat that we can row toward the Moon. And it is exceedingly dangerous to change boats after we have left the shore.

The one goal of realization.

Rama Krishna, the great Hindu God realized Saint of the nineteenth century, said that he had followed and mastered all the different forms of *yoga* and that they had all brought him to the one goal of *realization* (Sadhana), although along different paths. He also said that he had studied all the great religions, including two whole years spent in concentration on Jesus' teachings and in meditation on the Christos, "living all alone like a Christian anchorite in the famous woods of Panchabati,"[4] and he found that *they all led him to the same goal* of Advaita or identity with God. And the testimony of that great Saint who had experimentally followed each religion to its goal of realization should be conclusive.

The only heathen.

The practical application of this is that we need no missionaries to convert the "heathen." For certainly those who are following the Path of Realization and are worshipping the one God are not "heathen." The only heathen there are *those who refuse or neglect* to walk their path and worship their highest con-

---

[4] See *The Face of the Silence*, Mukerji, Chapter V.

cept of God. And we do not have to go outside of Chicago or any other city to find them. But *we do need missionaries* to teach mankind the beauties of their own religion, and above all, to recognize the One in the many, Unity in diversity, the Eternal in the ephemeral.

Creeds and dogmas.

Jesus did indeed say that His gospel should be preached unto all nations and peoples. But He also said: "Other sheep have I, which are not of this fold; them also I must bring, and they shall hear my voice (through their own religion); and there shall be one fold, and one shepherd."[5]

But did He enunciate a creed or formulate a dogma or establish a church? Certainly not. Those are all the offspring of man's speculations, often hundreds of years after the Master taught. His gospel was a realization of the Cosmic Christ-consciousness; the *identity of*

---
[5] *St. John*, X, 16.

all men in the Father, hence the universal Brotherhood of Man. That Christ-consciousness within was what St. Paul referred to when he said: "Until Christ be born in you." Jesus' only doctrine was Divine Love.

Love a cosmic power.

Now love is centripetal not centrifugal; is cohesive and constructive, not disruptive and destructive; is unifying, not separative. In fact love is the cohesive power of the universe. In the solar system it is that cohesive power, known as gravitation, which holds the planets in their orbits around the Sun. In the world of matter it is the cohesive power—called chemical affinity—that holds the molecules together to form objective material things. In the atom it is the cohesive power that holds the electrons and neutrons around the central proton.

In the family it is the affection that binds the children to the parents and to each other to form the family. If it is absent, the family naturally disintegrates because there is no cohesive force of love to hold it together. And if there is not, then it is the fault of the parents for not invoking it through prayer and meditation and allowing it to manifest in the family.

Like the electricity, love is always available, but we must take the time, thought and attention to turn it on, just as we must push the electric light button, if we would have spiritual light and love illumine our homes and our hearts. So do not blame the so-called "modern" children. It is the "modern" and God-less parents who are to blame. In the community love manifests as the civic spirit that binds the community or city together as an entity. Among nations it is patriotism and nationalism that makes the country one people. In races it is the blood tie that welds the various nations into a race. In humanity as a whole it is that spiritual quality of the species; that incarnated Ray of Divinity which distinguishes man from all other animals.

Mysticism solves the world's problems.

To be practical mystics and see how mysticism solves the world's problems, we must apply these few basic principles to our daily lives and contacts. From the one divine origin of mankind we deduce the basic Law of Brotherhood: that all men are brothers, no matter what their race, their color, or their creed. Indeed, as we identify ourselves with the One Cause we see our brothers as ourselves. With this first basic law understood and realized *and applied*, there could be no more war among nations, any more than there could be among members of a family who were manifesting that second great Law of Divine Love and living in and being ruled by love and affection. There would naturally be differences of opinion, but they are adjusted without fighting.

So should it be among nations. Each nation, like each organ of the body, has its own boundaries, its own life to live, and its own functions to perform. But none can live to themselves alone.

All are needed for the good of the whole. If one organ functions excessively or is feverish or ill, through the constructive application of the Law of Harmony, its activities are curbed and harmonized by constructive methods until it is brought into harmonious relationship with its fellows, and without injuring it or the others or destroying it or them. Therefore, if the principles of Christian Mysticism were applied there could be no war among the nations of mankind.

All classes necessary.

Just as each nation and race is necessary for the expression of humanity as a whole, so is each class within the nation necessary for the good of the whole.

Just as the head or the heart or the lungs or the hands and feet cannot be considered superior the one to the other, except relatively, for all are necessary for the manifestation of the complete man, so are all classes necessary for the complete manifestation of God in humanity. And since the health of the body is an important factor in the manifestation of the Soul through it, even the man who digs a ditch for a sewer to contribute to the health of a city is a factor which assists the manifestation of God on Earth. Hence his seemingly lowly labor is vitally important to the whole community and may even be regarded as service to God.[6]

Service and co-operation the Law of Life.

Therefore if the principles of Christian Mysticism are understood *and practised* there can be no class antagonism; for each class will recognize the necessity of performing its own tasks in the best possible manner and co-operating with all other classes in the most harmonious and constructive way. For we have seen that according to the cosmic laws of Sacrifice and of Love, *unselfish service* and *harmonious co-operation*, instead of selfish and *antagonistic competition* is the true Law of Life and happiness.

---

[6] See lesson *Work as Worship*, Curtiss.

If this involves planned and controlled production, distribution, and labor, then these things must come before our civilization is organized upon the lines of constructive cosmic forces which alone can make it endure. *The National Recovery Act* is now striving and working toward this goal of universal planned co-operation for the best good of all. And nearly every point in this plan which we broadcast before the Chamber of Commerce of Orlando, Florida, on March 29th, 1932,[7] has already been enacted into law or been proposed, and the other points must ultimately be added to complete the plan.

Simplified civilization.

In the light of this *law of unselfish co-operation* our whole system of living must be reorganized so as to make the demands of the outer life subservient to the manifestation of the inner life. For

---
[7] See lessons *Cosmic Causes of World Conditions and the Remedy*, Curtiss.

the material mechanics of living have become so complicated that we have become enslaved to our instruments of living. Our time and attention is so taken up with manipulating the so-called instruments of civilization that we have little time to live life itself. We are so diverted by the trivial details of the outer personality that we have no time nor attention left for communion with God, our Source of Life, or for the recognition and cultivation and expression of our Real Self or Soul.

From this standpoint "mass production" has proved a curse, in that it has developed new so-called needs which are really aids to self-indulgence, and have added to our enslavement to the complexities of living, instead of freeing us to enjoy the simplicities of life. We boast of labor-saving devices. But *why save labor?* Labor should be an avenue of creative self-expression and not blind toil. And we have "saved" so much of it that we do not know what to do with it, hence millions are unemployed.

Enlightenment, realization, service.

The solution which Christian Mysticism presents for the ills of our present civilization is *enlightenment, realization* and *manifestation* or *service*. For before we can properly organize our lives along cosmically constructive lines, we must be enlightened as to those lines or forces of causation. Then we must realize what life is all about, namely, where we came from, why we are here, and whither we are bound. We must realize that we incarnate here on Earth not to make money or to be hampered in the expression of our Divine Self by many complicated outer details and things to do. We come here to manifest as much of the inner Divine Self as our degree of unfoldment permits, and to learn to take the next step in that spiritual unfoldment. And we should make all our outer activities contribute to and yet be subordinate to that main object of life. If this be called putting our religion first, then so be it. For that is the most *practical* thing we can do; that is, put the accomplishment of our mission on Earth first in our lives.

In touch with Nature.

Simplifying life naturally calls for the gradual abandonment of city life, and the organizing of our lives in relatively small detached communities or villages of kindred Souls. And we should be in such close touch with the soil and with the creative forces of Nature that each family can expend at least a part of its creative energies in raising the majority of its food supply and in fashioning its fundamental instruments of living. In other words, we should so simplify our lives that each family would be relatively self-sustaining. Yet we need not scrap all modern conveniences of living, but make them subservient to our real needs and not merely generate new needs.

The plan of the hive.

Then our lives would be as normal and as well organized, yet as simple and self-sustaining, as that of the bee. If you will study the glass hives at the Century of Progress Exposition you will see that while from the outside the bees seem to be rushing to the hive in great haste and confusion, yet inside all is calm and peaceful and without haste or confusion. Each detail is carried out quietly and orderly by its own trained corps of workers until it is done thoroughly and efficiently *according to the plan of the hive* which is impressed upon the bees through the instinct of the group-soul of the species.

Follow our guidance.

Like the bee, we also have a plan for our lives to manifest and toward which we should direct all our activities, that our lives may become perfect cells in the honeycomb of life in which the nectar of God's light, life, and love may be stored up for our spiritual nourishment. That plan is impressed upon the Soul-consciousness and will be revealed step by step by God Himself through intuition to all who will listen and obey. We should therefore cultivate and follow the guidance of our intuition until our response to that guidance becomes just as habitual and instinctive as does the response of the bee to its guiding instinct.

Higher help needed.

But the Christian Mystic is one who also realizes that we do not have to work out our plan of life alone and unaided. In fact, we cannot fully accomplish our life's mission, learn its lessons, and redeem its mistakes in our own human strength; for that requires higher octaves of force than the mortal and human. And we know that *if we will only seek for it* we can have the help of *higher beings than the human*, just as the seeds can have the higher help of man to cultivate them. We can have the help, not only of our own Soul, our Spiritual Self, but also many classes of Invisible Helpers. But this help is not imposed upon us. *We must voluntarily seek for* and invoke and *then correlate* with it.

Heavenly Hierarchies.

Not only do our loved ones who have gone on ahead of us into the higher realms of life bring to us all the help, comfort, and guidance that their expanded consciousness and power and our receptivity permits, but both we and they also have still higher and greater helpers. For we have all the heavenly Hierarchies of Angelic Beings to aid and inspire, comfort and protect and sustain us to the extent that we call upon and tune in to their plane of consciousness and power.

And above and beyond all others we have the embodied aspect of God in the person of His Son—whether He be called the Christ, the Buddha, Krishna, or Horus in various religions. And He is so omnipresent and His consciousness is so omniscient and His love so all-inclusive and all-pervading that He is ever ready to respond to the call of every heart which sends up the wireless call of its aspiration, devotion, or need.

Contacting the Angels.

The reality of these angelic helpers and the mystery of our being able to contact them and receive their aid is testified to in all great religions in all ages.[8] In fact this mystic source of all life is the basis which underlies all religions and all worship. And the method of contacting these Angelic Beings we repeat is prayer, aspiration, and devotion. We do not need elaborate places of worship or other outer conditions, helpful as many such are, for as we said before, such contact is not a matter of outer things or even of mind, but of heart; not a matter of intellect but of worship.

In summarizing this address as we close we cannot do better than recall to your minds two stanzas of that well known hymn:

"Down from their home on high
Down through the starry sky.
Angels, descending fly,
While the Earth shaketh.

---

[8] For details see *Realms of the Living Dead*, Curtiss.

Roll they the stone away
From where the Savior lay.
Out into glorious day
His way He taketh."

Our true Resurrection.

And so may the angels of inspiration and Divine Guidance, spiritual understanding and illumination descend upon us here and now and roll away the stone of ignorance, of misunderstanding, and misconception, the stone of materialism, from our hearts and minds wherein we have kept the divine Christ-consciousness entombed these many years, that He may come forth and take His way with us in our lives. Thus shall we be resurrected from the old life of entombing personality and ascend into the consciousness of that larger life of the Spirit which is our heritage and our real home.

Thus does Christian Mysticism solve the world's problems through *enlightenment, realization,* and *manifestation* or service to Him and to our fellow men as to ourselves.

CHAPTER II

THE PATH OF DISCIPLESHIP

"The Path is the Path of Renunciation. . . . The renunciation must be the renunciation of the domination of the lower self and the disciplining and training of its desires and appetites." *The Voice of Isis, Curtiss, 296.*

"There is a Path which leads into the deep mysteries of God. There is a Path which leads into the world of Life Eternal. And its door is not of necessity the one called the death of the physical body. Yet it is in one sense death, but a death only of those things which we no longer need. It is on this Path that our life attains its ultimate end. It is here that we see the doors of the mighty Temple of Divine Life swing open. It is here that we hear the Voice of the Silence say to us: 'Put off thy shoes (the outer material coverings or material conceptions) from off thy feet (our understanding), for the ground on which thou standest is holy ground.'" *Harriette Augusta Curtiss.*

Spiritual advance in former times.

At first thought the term Path of Discipleship, the Path which leads to a realization of the mystery of the relation between God and man, suggests a course of severe discipline and asceticism. For that was the idea commonly connected with the thought of spiritual advance which has been handed down from the Dark Ages.

The Path of Discipleship is, indeed, a difficult and strenuous one, firstly, because a disciple must be one who is not merely a vague follower of his Master or his chosen ideal, but is one who endeavors to *embody that ideal* in all the affairs of his daily life. Secondly, the Path is difficult because the disciple is definitely seeking to advance more rapidly than the rate afforded by the slow and sluggish evolutionary path of racial evolution which gradually sweeps the great mass of humanity along through the ages, ultimately sweeping them to the foot of the Mount of Attainment[1] where they must then consciously begin to climb its heights. This Path is difficult because the disciple must accomplish, in the few years of this incarnation, the advance for which the race requires ages.

---

[1] See lesson *The Mount of Attainment*, Curtiss.

Discipleship is a steep ascent.

The Path is also difficult because the disciple must rise above the crowd and enter into, and be affected by, and respond to, new and higher octaves of vibration. For he is starting out on a higher round on the Spiral of Life[2] where he must again meet the same problems and face the same tests that he has met and passed on the lower rounds years ago. Here he must prove that those former lessons were really learned and that their powers were really built into his character. But he now faces these tests with a more sensitive organism which reacts more strongly to them. Yet he also has the greater strength gained by passing those tests at the lower stages of his unfoldment.

The preparation for meeting these tests of life and the temptations of the flesh with a more sensitive and more easily responsive organism was formerly made by seeking to avoid them through

---

[2] See *The Message of Aquaria*, Curtiss, Chapter XVI.

retiring from the world in monastery or convent, in the forest or the jungle, and leading an ascetic life. And this same idea is still held in the Orient and in many churches today in connection with advanced spiritual teachings and attainments. But we hold that such conceptions arise from a misunderstanding of the nature and purpose of man and his bodies.

Starting out from the Father's home.

Those who have read the books or followed the Teachings of this Order know that our bodies are not ourselves: that *we are not mere mortals*, but that the Real Self of us is a divine and glorious Spiritual Being whose home is in the spiritual world. But since it is the will of the Father that His life, His consciousness, and His love shall be manifested consciously in all the worlds of manifestation, from the heavenly homeworld down through all the intervening states and stages of manifestation until this dense world of matter is reached, to us, His enlightened children, is given the great task of demonstrating our Divinity by descending into this material world to manifest here on Earth the divine and godlike qualities and powers which we inherit from Him.

The personality necessary.

But to accomplish this mission we must don garments that are suitable to this dense material world in which we are to work. We are like a diver who has to put on a heavy, cumbersome diving suit (our animal body) and have his feet (our understanding) heavily weighted with lead (our materialistic conceptions). Such a suit is so terribly hampering to the diver that he can accomplish only a small fraction of the work he could do out of water without it. Yet it is the only means by which he can accomplish anything at all down in the mud of the sea bottom. And as the diver receives his supply of life-giving air from above, so must we rely upon and correlate with the Breath of the Spirit to sustain our spiritual life while we are manifesting here in the depths of the sea of materiality. And just as the diver must respond to, and be guided by, the signals and directions given him from his attendants above for his safety and accomplishment, so must we respond to and obey our guidance from above.

Natural desires.

But, unlike the diving suit, the garment we have to don to manifest on Earth is not a mere inert material covering, not a mere mechanical instrument which automatically conforms itself to our every movement, wish, and desire. It is a living organism, the most highly evolved organism of the animal kingdom, the human body. Consequently this animal body has all the functions, appetites, passions, and desires that any animal has. And it is just here that misunderstanding of the whole plan of manifestation has led to the practice of asceticism.

Because this animal body of ours requires training and control, the erroneous conclusion has been reached that the surest way to control its troublesome activities is to fast and starve them into submission and ultimately kill them out. But such a process is not control. It is only devitalization. It is not mastery. It is only emasculation.

Eastern vs. Western methods.

How, then, are we to accomplish the real training, the real disciplining, the real mastery of this our animal instrument of manifestation? It is the methods used to accomplish this end that constitute the training and discipline of the Path of Discipleship, whether they be the medieval and Oriental path of asceticism or the Christian Mystic path of perfection, mastery, and joyous use of all man's God-given powers as avenues of expression for, and under the guidance of, the Real Self.

Therein lies the fundamental difference between the Eastern and the Western, the Oriental and the Occidental, conceptions of the Path. The Eastern or ascetic ideal holds that not only are the natural functions of the animal body and the desires of the human personality a handicap to the manifestation of the Real Self, but are almost a curse; that God made a great mistake when He clothed His children with such a hampering instrument of manifestation, and hence the best thing to do is to have as little to do with it as possible. On the other hand, the Christian Mystic ideal is that God knew exactly what He was about when He evolved[3] this animal body and gave it to our incarnating Souls to use as His advanced representatives here on Earth.

Guidance from within.

Our main idea in the training of the personality and its animal body therefore is to teach it to respond to and be guided by the Real Self within as readily and as instinctively as it responds to the vibrations from without and the sensations

---

[3] See *The Truth About Evolution and the Bible*, Curtiss.

from below. We must teach our human personality that if it will obey our ideals and follow our directions it will not only be far healthier, but also far happier, and will have greater satisfaction in living its life than if it merely seeks unlimited gratification of its animal instincts. It will be healthier because the normal condition of the incarnating Soul is one of peace and harmony. Hence the more we strive to express the ideals and principles of the Soul life, the more peaceful, harmonious, and happy, and hence the more healthful, will our lives become. And we will be more satisfied because we will govern our reactions to the outer world by the vibrations of the Divine Self within. For we must remember that it is not outer persons, things, and conditions that upset us and make our lives inharmonious, but *our reaction to them*. We should also remember that true satisfaction cannot be found in outer conditions, possessions, or things. We experience true soul-satisfying satisfaction only as we respond to and manifest the Real Self within.

Control our reactions.

What is it that most disturbs the peace and harmony of our lives? It is our reaction to, and expression of, our inharmonious and destructive emotions, such as irritability, impatience, anger, hatred, lust, fear, envy, jealousy, selfishness, etc. All such emotions have been scientifically proven to produce chemical changes or toxins in the blood which poison the whole body. In view of this, what can we do to prevent the generation and expression of these destructive emotions?

Firstly, we must firmly fix in our minds that *we are not mortals,* but are *spiritual beings* who, in our Real Selves, have no annoyance, resentment, or anger. Neither are we envious of the possessions of others nor jealous of their attainments. For we came down to Earth to express our own attainments, and we really need only such possessions as will best enable us to manifest those attainments. All else would be an added responsibility and a burden which would occupy much of our time, attention, and creative forces and hence would hamper our highest expression.

Secondly, we must realize that to give way to impatience, resentment, anger, etc., opens our minds to the thought currents of such things which have been generated by the whole community in which we live. By giving them expression we open the door of our minds and allow the accumulated community currents to flow in and find expression through us. Thus they sweep us off our feet into disruptive outbursts which far exceed the trivial causes which started them and which are greatly in excess of anything we intended or thought of expressing.

The remedy.

Therefore the remedy is to grasp the basic idea that all such inharmonious manifestations belong merely to the human personality and not to our Real Self; that they express selfishness, personal vanity, or the passions and desires of the animal self, and are not worthy of being allowed to find expression through us. Such expression can be prevented by checking them as soon as their vibration starts to manifest by immediately turning our attention to the opposite emotion to which we do wish to give expression, and feed that constructive emotion by concentrating upon it and giving it expression.

This complies with the command of Jesus to, "Resist not evil, but overcome evil with good." For to resist evil we must recognize it and give it our attention. And anything we focus our attention upon we feed and give power over us. Therefore, if we focus our attention upon giving expression to the constructive emotion we feed it and give it power over us, and thus overcome the evil, first by weakening it by the withdrawal of our attention and thought currents which feed it, and then overwhelming it by the power of the good that we have created.

One of our basic principles of life must therefore be never to allow anything to upset or interfere with the happy and harmonious manifestation of the inner peace, poise, love, and rhythm of our Real or Divine Self. Nothing in the outer life is of sufficient importance to be allowed to upset the calm poise of our inner harmony.

Positive radiating centers.

Nothing can do so if every morning on awakening we fervently repeat our *Prayer to the Divine Indweller*. "Welcome, O Lord of Life and Love and Beauty! Thou who art myself and yet art God! And dwell in this body of flesh, radiating all the beauty of holiness and perfection, that the flesh may out picture all that Thou art within." Thus we will charge our minds with the realization that we are to manifest, just for that one day at a time, the inner peace, joy, and happiness of our Divine Indweller. As we thus realize the Divine within that is struggling for expression through ourselves and through others, we will be tolerant of the mistakes and annoying actions of others who are less evolved than ourselves, and hence are less under the guidance and control of the Real Self, and will not allow them to upset us.

If we are also kind and unselfish in little things and try to divert the inharmonious manifestations of others by refusing to react to them and by turning them aside with a smile or by changing the subject and diverting their attention from them, then the big things, the big tests and temptations and trials, will readily be recognized for what they are and be conquered. In other words, we will accomplish far more good in the world, both for ourselves and others, when we make ourselves positive centers for the radiation of cheer, joy, happiness, and peace which elicit similar responses from others, than when we strive to be austere saints or to appear learned, superior, or pious.

Realization of the Presence.

But even though we earnestly strive to be such radiant centers of constructive and inspiring forces, while we are training ourselves to react only constructively to outer conditions, persons, and forces, there are times when we need outside help or rather inside help: a power greater than that of our human personality, namely, the help of the Christ within. For to this ever-present Power we can always turn for help the instant we find ourselves likely to give way to vibrations and emotions and thoughts which we do not wish to express. And one instant's response to His indwelling peace, poise, power, and love, an instant's response to His command, "Peace. Be still," is sufficient to calm the turbulent sea of our emotions and our reactions to the outer conditions. For there are no storms which His power cannot quell and no conditions which He cannot dominate and conquer if we will but remember to ask His aid and permit Him to manifest through us.

The more often we realize that He is ever present with and within us continually, in all our work, in all our play, in all our trials and temptations; and the more often we consciously turn to Him for help and guidance, the more do His vibrations find expression through us and help us to conquer, perfect, and master this human personality of ours and all its reactions. Thus do we not kill out or emasculate it, but continually improve it as an instrument for the ever greater manifestation of our Real Self within.

There must be rigid discipline of the personality and its body, yes. But it must be the discipline and control due not to fear of penalty nor to ambition for personal attainment, but to a glad and joyous response to the guidance of the Christ within.

The Path of expression.

The Path of Discipleship, as we conceive it, is, therefore, one of consciously striving to follow the guidance of the Divine within in all the affairs of life.

It is the Path, not of suppression and killing out, but of recognition *and mastery* of all our forces and faculties in their proper place and for their highest purposes. For they are built into our various bodies by the Father to enable us to express our Divine Selfhood and do His will the more perfectly here on Earth, even as it is done in heaven. It is the Path of constructive and harmonious expression; of happiness and joyous radiation of our highest conception of the Divine Self within.

And since happiness is what all mankind is consciously or unconsciously seeking, this Path of the practice of the positive radiation of our highest and best is the surest way to its attainment. And since a disciple is a devoted exemplar of his Master's teachings, the proof of our sincerity and devotion will be the degree of our manifestation of our highest ideals and our inner guidance. And as we manifest these, the radiation of our lives will be a source of inspiration, uplift and happiness to all we contact, and will stimulate them also to seek out and follow this higher, mystical, constructive, and joyous Path of Discipleship.

CHAPTER III

Illumination[1]

"I am the way, the truth, and the life: no man cometh unto the Father, but by me." *St. Matthew*, XIV, 6.

"I am the Ego which is seated in the hearts of all beings: I am the beginning, the middle, and the end of all existing things." *The Bhagavad-Gita*, Chapter X.

Practical directions for Illumination.

Pupils are asking continually for some formula, some prescribed "practical" thing to do to advance their spiritual evolution, complaining that they have read and studied all forms of philosophy and are now ready for something "definite." Because of this widespread demand there have sprung up on every hand those who are professing to give "practical" directions that shall lead the pupil into Illumination and give him miraculous powers.

---

[1] From *The Voice of Isis*, Curtiss, 378.

On the other hand, an equally large number are writing that they have studied various systems, spent large sums of money for "advanced teachings," received the lessons of the inner section of many organizations, have passed through many mysterious degrees of various societies with high-sounding titles, and yet find their spiritual hunger unappeased, the net result being a mass of so-called formulas and a greater amount of discouragement.

Others turn to the Wisdom Religion, supposing that it has to do with the development of psychic powers and the performance of magical rites, but, in truth, it has primarily to do with the development of the Christ-force within and the showing of it forth in the life. So-called magic is dual. If it is the result of the recognition and outward manifestation of the Christ-within it is White Magic and right; if the result of seeking for power or personal stature it becomes Black Magic and evil. Therefore, to all these classes of seekers, as well as to many other hungry hearts, we bring the old, old message, "I (the Christ-within) am the way, the truth, and the life: no man cometh unto the Father, but by me."

Union with the Divine.

What is it that all are thus seeking? It is so-called Illumination, yet few there be who have any realization of what this means. We have considered various phases of this Illumination in previous lessons,[2] and we will try herein to show what the real Illumination is and how it is attained. Illumination is the perfect blending of the self with the Divine or the Christ-light, so that Divine Wisdom can guide every thought and act of the mortal man and the Light of Divinity can shed its radiance over the entire life.

The result of spiritual force in each life.

When it is remembered that the Bible story of the Christ is the most complete and all-embracing narrative ever written,

---
[2] See *The Voice of Isis*, Curtiss.

not of the man Jesus or even of God, but a synthetic picture of the Son of God—the emanation from the Father, the Christ-force in humanity or the Word made flesh—which symbolizes the various steps each Soul must pass through and conquer, it becomes quite plain that as this union with the Divine takes place, the life of the disciple must manifest greater conceptions of Truth. The whole mysterious transformation must be a growth similar to the gradual assimilation of the life-giving constituents of the Sun by the plant, until the full fruition or indwelling of the life-force is accomplished in the fruit.

When we grasp this thought firmly we will understand that we must and shall do the works of our Father in exact proportion to our ability to make the correlation with Him, just as the plant does the works of its father, the Sun—first as the blade, then the ear, then the full corn in the ear. Therefore there can be no rigid observances laid down for the attainment of perfection any more than there can be for the perfection of every individual plant. There can, however, be practices that develop the *will*, awaken the *intuition*, and stimulate *aspiration*, and there are environments which will foster spiritual growth, i.e., within the ranks of any spiritual movement whose teachings satisfy your Soul hunger, but these have been fully covered in other lessons. To the average twentieth century student the effort to conquer himself is quite sufficient to develop his will, and the only stimulant necessary is a burning, ardent seeking for a realization of the Christ-love.

Assimilation necessary.

Illumination, however, can never be attained through the mere reading of lessons or the observance of rules. It must be the result of a vital force that comes into each life. The gardener may prepare the soil, tend and water a plant, but the plant itself must assimilate the light and force of the Sun and literally transmute them into living tissue within its body, ere the blossom or the fruit can appear. So it is with the Illumination that each Soul is seeking. Only the Christ-force, not only talked about and in a sense realized, but literally absorbed and built into living tissue in the flesh, the mind, and the Spirit, can bring about this mystical union. It is the Christ and the Christ alone who is "the Way, the Truth, and the Life."

Development of the personality.

As certain plants gather from the Sun-force the power to produce poisons, so can man, by using for his own personal ends the godlike powers with which he can identify himself, produce evil. We do not create power, we only identify our consciousness with the Divine which is the source of all power, just as we might attach a wire to a dynamo and obtain power. Of the Divine Self alone it is said, "All power is given unto thee in heaven and earth." This is literally true. All power is ours if we identify ourselves with the Divine, and the synthesis of all power is the ability to merge the personality into the Divine, or become one with the Father through the Christ. This gives all power because, having accomplished this, all things are possible.

The choice is man's.

As man is endowed with free-will, he can choose to take either the Right Hand Path, merge the human into the Divine and use his God-power to do the work of his Father-in-heaven, or he can graft his God-power onto the stalk of personality and, by making the intellect alone his guiding star, deliberately forswear his Father-in-heaven and become a child of evil (or the devil) and do the works of his father, the devil—the concentrated force of man's wrong thoughts, acts, and creations, the perverted reflection of the Good Law (the Lord) on Earth.

By refusing to let the light of the Divine penetrate farther than the intellect, he closes the door of his heart and allows the Light to illumine only his human brain which, without the guidance of his heart, permits evil to manifest, especially intellectual and spiritual pride, which are the most subtle and insidious of all evils. Therefore, to teach mankind how to unfold inner faculties and how to use their power for personal ends would be quite as reprehensible as for a gardener to propagate, in a garden devoted to raising food for man, some poisonous vine which the gardener knew the very richness of the soil, the sunshine, and the cultivation would cause to grow and, finally, either destroy the food or impregnate it with poison.

This is why the inner teachings of the sacred Mysteries are given only to the few. It is no Being who gives; it is the blossom of the Soul which opens and receives the Light of Illumination, as the rose unfolds its petals to the light of the Sun. If you do not receive this Light, know well that the blossoming time has not arrived for you. Had it arrived no one could withhold the Light from you.

Natural unfoldment.

When the Divine mystery of the indwelling of the Christ has taken place in the Soul and the disciple has begun to realize in a vital, living way, that the overshadowing of his Divine Self is a real blending or indwelling, then the works of his Father will unfold within him just as the blade, the ear, and the full corn in the ear unfold in the plant. Then, and then only, is he ready for the inner teaching; for he must be trained to put forth his blossoms in the manner best for humanity. Each step gained must not only show in the life, but the powers that go with that step must also manifest.

If we control one selfish trait which before held us captive, we may know that we have taken a real step upward. And the first and greatest of all magical powers to be attained by the pupil is the magical power of controlling himself, of day after day *mastering the little things*, with no heroics, perhaps with no one to commend him or realize that he is making any effort, yet still controlling his little tempers, his little impatiences, little acts of selfishness, his tendency to criticize and all the little, trifling things he knows are wrong, but which seem too petty to be worth mentioning.

Hidden obstacles.

Let no pupil ask for special lessons until these little things are in a measure conquered, for the building of these little lessons into his life is the most "practical" formula that can be given him. And if there is anyone who has thus assimilated the Christ and grown to live the Christ-life, who has gained the power of looking at the self, who has fulfilled the injunction, "Know thyself," yet who says he still lacks Illumination, let him know well that there is some hidden corner of his heart or life into which the Light is not able to penetrate, some closed door which he refuses to open. To him we would say: Look deeper and meditate in the Silence and pray for a knowledge of thyself. At the same time go forth and help to bring the Light to some other Soul, for in so doing, in some part of your nature you will find that which keeps out the full radiance of the Christ-light. Let him "Learn to look intelligently into the hearts of men. Regard most earnestly your own heart. For through your own heart comes the one light which can illuminate life, and make it clear to your eyes."[3]

Intellectual and Heart Development necessary.

Occult formulas are more apt to emphasize self-satisfaction and self-righteousness than to help toward self-mastery. John the Baptist had been educated in all the law of the Mysteries, had lived apart from the world in the caves of the wilderness, had fed on locusts and wild honey, and had spent his life following out the most rigid formularies of the Essenes, yet Jesus said: "Verily I say unto you, Among them that

---
[3] *Light on the Path*, Collins, Part II, Rules 10-12.

are born of women there hath not arisen a greater than John the Baptist: notwithstanding he that is least in the kingdom of heaven is greater than he."[4] This means that the very humblest person who has correlated with the Christ within—which is entering the kingdom of heaven—is greater than even a great intellectual teacher such as John the Baptist.

A short cut.

Both intellectual development and heart development *are necessary*, but, if the heart is first developed and a conscious union made with the Christ within, all things are revealed unto you. This is, as it were, the short cut to Mastery.

It is a singular fact that none of the Great Teachers—Krishna, Buddha, Jesus, etc.—ever wrote a word, or were, in Their day, looked upon as great intellectual teachers, but the example of Their lives lives in the world to this day,

---

[4] *St. Mattew*, XI, 11.

and can never die, because They made this divine correlation, literally manifesting God in the flesh. It is neither the words you speak nor the routine of your life that affects the world, but something more. *It is the power of that which is "the way, the truth, and the life."* In other words, both that which you teach and the example of your life must prove conclusively that it is the Christ within you that worketh through you both to will and to do.

It must not be a mere lip-service, it must be so true and so convincing that it will radiate from you rather than be a garment assumed before the world or a mere intellectual cloak that blinds your own eyes, for the Christ within you must be the Truth as well as the Way and the Life.

Recapitulation.

If there is any doubt left in regard to the Path we point out to reach this attainment, we will briefly recapitulate.

Think only constructively if you desire spiritual growth.

Do cheerfully and well the duty that lies nearest.

Conquer the little faults as they show themselves.

Never let a day close without its period of self-examination, meditation, and communion with the Divine before going to sleep.

Do unto others as ye would that others should do unto you.

Learn to love in its truest and grandest sense.

Do not criticize others, even though your criticism seems just; for to do so you must dwell mentally in the conditions you criticize.

Be not afraid to face and recognize *your own* faults.

At the same time be not discouraged.

Have perfect confidence in your power ultimately to conquer through the Christ within.

For the voice of the Christ declares, "Lo, I am with you alway, even unto the end of the world."

CHAPTER IV

THE MYSTIC CHRIST

"By revelation he made known unto me the mystery; (as I wrote afore in a few words, whereby, when ye read, ye may understand my knowledge in the mystery of Christ)." *Ephesians*, III, 3-4.

"I am crucified with Christ; nevertheless I live; yet not I, but Christ liveth in me: and the life which I now live in the flesh I live by the faith of the Son of God, who loved me, and gave himself for me." *Galatians*, II, 20.

Men still seek spiritual guidance.

DESPITE the complaint that the world is becoming irreligious, and that men are deserting the churches for the golf links, the tennis court, and the motor car, "a list of questions sent to one hundred and twenty of the most prominent business men of Toledo" (U.S.A.) disclosed the fact that "there is a pathetic yearning for a sufficient faith" in religious teachings and an astonishing amount of "deep and serious thought evidently given the subject" among business men. "Two impressions are made upon the propounder of the questions. One is that men are interested as much as ever in the history of the world, in the great religious questions regarding life and destiny. The other is that never has there been greater need, nor greater opportunity, for ministers to present intelligently, rationally, and earnestly the fundamental truths of Christianity. Men are hungrily seeking for true guidance in things spiritual."[1]

Intuitive perception of spiritual things.

With all this desire for guidance, there could be no startling denials of doctrines commonly cherished by the Church were the esoteric, mystic, and spiritual interpretations of those doctrines presented instead of the literal, materialistic, and historical. The day has passed when the Church can arbitrarily place a certain interpretation upon the spiritual mysteries

---

[1] Rev. George R. Wallace in *The Advance*, Chicago.

and say to her followers, "Thus must ye believe." For the consciousness of spiritual freedom is sweeping the world, and there is an inner heart-knowledge which refuses to respond to that which does not vibrate to its intuitive revelation of truth.

Any presentation of truth must touch the heart and square itself with the experiences of daily life, else it will be rejected in this age whose slogan is "Efficiency." As well might we expect the world to accept and cling to medieval conceptions of science as to expect it to be satisfied with dogmas founded upon interpretations of the scriptures made during the Dark Ages. Unless religious teachings, like all others, can advance, expand, and successfully solve the practical problems of the age, they must inevitably be discarded and left behind.

The historic and the Mystic Christ.

This is especially true if the teachings pertaining to the Christ are made synonymous with the personality of Jesus as an historical character. For, in reality, the Christ which is worshipped by Christendom to-day is not the historic personality portrayed by the gospels, but the Mystic Christ as set forth in the *Epistles* of Paul. The great discrepancy, between the two presentations has long been a puzzle to biblical scholars and has caused such confusion in the minds of thoughtful students that many, despairing a reasonable solution that would satisfy both their reason and their heart-hunger for spiritual food, turn from such stones of material conceptions offered them as bread.

The difficulty arises through a failure to distinguish between the Mystic Christ-principle, which "hath shined in our hearts, to give the light of knowledge of the glory of God," and the personality of the teacher Jesus who manifested an individualization of this force to a superlative degree. This distinction is so plainly made throughout the New Testament that only the decadence of knowledge concerning the Mysteries and the lack of training in esoteric philosophy as a requirement for the ministry can account for the utter ignoring of it and all that it implies.

The historic example still needed by some.

In reality there is no discrepancy between the Gospels and the Epistles, once the philosophy of the Mystic Christ is understood, for Jesus taught it as distinctly as did Paul. Broadly, the Gospel picture purposely presents the manifestation of the Christ-force in humanity as exemplified in the symbolic life of Jesus—while the picture given by the *Epistles* represents the same force as existing in the higher mystic realms and manifesting to the heart of man through his awakened spiritual faculties. In one sense the Gospel picture is meant to inspire those whose spiritual development requires a physical embodiment and a personal, historic example after which to pattern their lives. These are but children in spiritual understanding, to whom the beautiful embodiment of the Christ within the manifested Jesus, the Man of Sorrows, forms a picture with great emotional appeal. If they stop there, however, and are satisfied with the personality of the human teacher, they never really find the Christ as a personal, religious experience, nor do they even touch the hem of His garment. They worship but a picture and are doomed to disappointment and sorrow, for some day they must see their human Christ-ideal crucified, cast down, and destroyed.[2]

Each of you, as you grow in spiritual grace and unfoldment, must have more than a physical ideal, however perfect; for you are both body and spirit, human and Divine, and you cannot understand, describe, or realize your real Mystic Self, with all its strange longings and promptings, its flashes of illumination, its glimpses of glory, until you have outgrown the limitations which inhere in a human ideal of the Mystic Christ. Because of this duality there is no one, be

---

[2] By historical research, higher criticism, etc.

he ever so stern a materialist, who in crucial moments when self-analysis is forced upon him, can deny that there is a great unknown region of mystery within him; indefinable longings, the urge of the Christ-force within struggling for recognition and expression.

The Mystic Christ must be born in you.

The Pauline picture is for those who need no historic personality as a model; those who open wide the doors of their hearts at the knock of the Mystic Christ; who can respond to the downpouring of Divine Love and through a divine ecstasy can enter into the higher realms of spiritual consciousness where the powers of the human mind are transcended and where they grasp those things which can only be spiritually discerned; those things which are "revealed unto his holy apostles and prophets by the Spirit."[3]

In another sense both pictures are necessary. The literal, personal example or

---
[3] *Ephesians*, III, 5.

letter of the law, is not satisfying to the awakened Soul. It must be animated and illumined by the vision of the Mystic Christ, else it degenerates into hero worship or idolatry. On the other hand, the mystic conception must have its physical embodiment—Christ must be born in you—in the life of the disciple—or it is but a passing vision. Both are necessary. Just as the physical Sun is necessary to focus and make physical the forces whose origin is in the Spiritual Sun, so must there be a physical embodiment to focus and make manifest upon the physical plane the Mystic Christ-force.

The Christ is the creative aspect of Divinity.

Jesus the man was an Avatar who, as He himself says, "came down from heaven, not to do mine own will, but the will of him that sent me," while the Mystic Christ is not a personality, but a Divine Essence. It is a spiritual emanation from the Godhead, the Son of God or the Godhead in its creative aspect;

that mystic Power or Principle which fructifies and animates all manifestations of life. It is the Divine Creative Force, a great stream of life-giving, creative Essence which manifests in all things on all planes as the animating Principle of the One Life. In Nature it is focused in and through the physical Sun, for only as the Sun pours out its life-giving, fructifying power—sheds its symbolic blood—can the One Life manifest in the various forms of Nature and evolve them to perfection. In the physical universe it is the same animating Principle that flamed out from the Godhead in the beginning when the Elohim said, "Let there be light." And it is this same mystic, creative Light which must enter the chaos of your outer life, even as it did the chaos of the solar system, ere your life can begin its conscious spiritual evolution. All the physical and mental evolution is but a preparation for this new and higher step. Witness Paul's confirmation of this view. "For God, who commanded the light to shine out of darkness, hath shined in our hearts, to give the light of the knowledge of the glory of God in the face of Jesus Christ."[4]

Its center in man is the heart.

Just as the creative Christ-force is focused in physical Nature in the Sun, so must it have its focal center in man. This center is primarily in the heart, and since the heart contains focal points connected with all the sacred centers in man, from that great center the Christ-light is reflected into the corresponding sub centers in all his bodies—in the physical body in the sun-center, the solar plexus; in the psychic body in the pineal gland; in the mental body in the power of intuition; in the spiritual body in the spiritual heart-center. The Christ-force therefore, is the animating Power back of all life and evolution—physical, mental, psychic, spiritual. "It is the life essence of this Law (love)—the Christ-force—which has overcome the world or

---
[4] 11 *Corinthians*, IV, 6.

which has brought about the physical evolution of the planet. Hence it must also bring about your spiritual evolution and bring to perfection all who choose to work in harmony with the Christ."[5] In Nature it is the unquenchable urge toward perfection which adapts the organism to its environment. Among men it is the divine urge toward union with God; the effort "to bring the divine within them into harmony with the divine in the universe," as the mystic philosopher Plotinus expresses it.

St. Paul refers to the Mystic Christ.

St. Paul, who is universally admitted to be the organizer and founder of the Christian Church, through whose teachings the followers of Jesus were raised from an obscure Jewish sect to a powerful spiritual movement and through whose influence the name was changed from Nazarenes to Christians, distinctively sets forth only the Mystic Christ. He

---

[5] *The Voice of Isis*, Curtiss, 214.

knew nothing of the personality of Jesus and never confused the historic character with the Christ-principle which had illumined him. When he says: "But we speak the wisdom of God in a mystery, even the hidden wisdom,"[6] he shows that he taught only the esoteric Mystic Christ of the Mysteries—into which he had been initiated among the Greeks—but with that intellectual ideal illumined by the personal, spiritual experience symbolized by his miraculous conversion (initiation). Like many a scholar to this day, learned in esoteric philosophy and sincerely worshipping his ideal of the Mystic Christ, Paul felt justified in persecuting the followers of the poor Hebrew cult whose teachings he considered were personalizing and therefore degrading the Mystic Christ ideal which he worshipped. He proved the sincerity of his worship, however, by changing his whole life when the Spirit revealed to him that he could not despise another's highest ideals—even

---

[6] *I Corinthians*, II, 7.

though seemingly low to him—or persecute the followers of another teacher, without crucifying his own Mystic Christ.

Paul never met Jesus.

Paul not only never knew Jesus the man, but he did not even study under the apostles; in fact, never met them until after he had been preaching the doctrine of the Mystic Christ for three years, and then he only abode with them fifteen days.[7] Twelve years later, when he next met them, he came not to learn about their personal teacher Jesus, but to teach them the doctrine of the Mystic Christ. More than this, Paul states: "I certify to you, brethren, that the gospel which was preached of me is not after man. For I neither received it of man, *neither was I taught it,* but by the revelation of Jesus Christ."[8] This is another evidence that it was the Christ of the Mysteries, the informing, spiritual, creative Principle

---

[7] *Galatians*, I, 17-18.
[8] *Ibid.*, I, 11-12.

which overshadows and illumines every heart that will open the door and let it in, to which Paul referred.

It is not the evolution of civilization that brings the mystic knowledge, far from it. Many an untutored savage is a member of the Mystic Brotherhood of the Elect because he has attained some degree of the Christ-consciousness and dwells in the mystic realm of ideality which makes all else unreal, no matter how incapable of expressing his vision his intellectual faculties may be.

Christ in you.

It cannot be the personality of Jesus of which Paul speaks when he says: "My little children, of whom I travail in birth again until Christ be formed in you,"[9] but of the awakening of the Christ-consciousness, the birth of the Mystic Christ in the heart of each disciple. And it is during this critical period in the evolution of the Soul that every spiritual

---
[9] *Galatians*, IV, 19; III, 27.

teacher is greatly concerned about his disciples. It is this Mystic Christ which the disciple "puts on" when he receives his great illumination or baptism. "For as many of you as have been baptized into Christ have put on Christ."[9] It is this same mystic power which urges Paul "to make all men see what is the fellowship of the mystery, which from the beginning of the world hath been hid in God, who created all things, by Jesus Christ."[10]

Christ's flesh and blood.

It is this mystic, informing, vivifying Principle, manifesting in and through Him, to which Jesus referred when He said: "I am the living bread which came down from heaven: if any man eat of this bread, he shall live forever: and the bread that I will give is my flesh, which I will give for the life of the world. . . . Whoso eateth my flesh, and drinketh my blood, hath eternal life."[11]

---

[10] *Ephesians*, III, 9.
[11] *St. John*, VI, 51, 54.

Assimilation necessary.

Manifestly such statements could not apply to any human flesh and blood nor even to an historical personality, but were used figuratively for that immortal, universal, mystic Principle which the personality of Jesus embodied. As the Sun's rays come down from heaven to bring the life-force of the Sun to Earth, that all Nature, which eats of it or assimilates it, may have life, so He whom we call Jesus, a perfected spiritual Being or Avatar,[12] descended from heaven and took upon Himself a fleshly body that He might bring the Light of the Spiritual Sun—the Mystic Christ-force—into humanity, that whoso eats of His flesh—or assimilates the lesson of such a physical manifestation—may have eternal life.

Eternal life cannot be obtained by merely observing or studying spiritual truths, for they must be eaten and assimilated into the nature, built into the character, made a part of the life—just as physical food must be assimilated to be

---

[12] *The Voice of Isis*, Curtiss, Chapter X.

built into the body—and manifest as love, tolerance, charity, brotherhood, and purity, ere you have truly eaten of the body of the Christ. Only as the Christ-force is embodied in you can you have eternal life.

Moral models insufficient.

As the perfected physical embodiment of the Christ is the mystic bread, so is the blood of the Christ the spiritual life-principle of that body. To grow spiritually it is not enough merely to model your lives upon the physical manifestation—the body—merely to lead ethical and morally blameless lives, but you must also drink of the blood; drink in that spiritual creative Power or Divine Life-force which shall re-create you, which shall make your lives not merely automatic moral models, but dynamic, radiant centers of force for good, vibrant with that creativeness whose very emanations shall fructify and awaken in everything you contact an answering vibration and a quickened life. "It is the spirit that quickeneth; the flesh profiteth nothing." There must be an infusion of the creative life-force of the Christ into the personality until it becomes one with the Mystic Christ.

First steps.

The first step in this attainment is to open your eyes. Pray for realization. Pray for understanding. Then there must come a sweeping away of old conditions, a deliberate turning away from the allurements of the outer life and at the same time an opening of your heart to the Mystic Christ. Refuse to allow your spiritual growth to be hampered either by thoughts of poverty, loneliness, sickness, or inharmony. These things may come, but your life is hid in the Mystic Christ and they cannot overcome or move you. As you turn away from the old conditions which have bound you so long, seek diligently in your hearts for that which holds you to them. How often have you said to yourselves, "Why am I eating of the husks with the swine?

Why am I in this far country of physical conceptions and material thoughts when my Father's home in the mystic realms is full of love, of food, of fine raiment and of welcome awaiting me?"

And the cry of the Mystic Christ answers you from out the ages, "Take eat; this is my body. . . . Drink ye all of it; for this is my blood. . . . Behold, I stand at the door and knock; if any man hear my voice, and open the door, I will come in to him, and will sup with him, and he with me."[13]

Glimpses of glory.

Oh! the love that has waited so long! And yet, were it not that, again and again as the ages roll on and on and your Souls clothe themselves in fleshly bodies, you have taken up the old mystic teachings, have responded to the great love that was yearning over you, you would not be where you are to-day. Often, in your long evolutionary journey have you caught glimpses of the light and the

---

[13] *Revelation*, III, 20.

glory, have heard the tinkling of the cymbals and the dancing of feet in the halls of your Father's home. Many a time have you stopped to listen. Many a time have your eyes been opened and you have seen the glory. Yet you have slept on. You have said, "A little more sleep. A little more struggle. Another earthly pilgrimage and then, bye and bye, I will arise and return to my Father." Many of you, alas, have laid down to rest by the wayside. You have slept while the procession marched by. The Lord of Life has passed you in the night while your eyelids were heavy with sleep.

Awake!

Again today this same Mystic Christ comes to you as the herald of the dawn of the new Aquarian Age and says: "I bring to you a message of peace, of encouragement and love. I call to you to awake! Awake! Sleep no longer! Determine to shake off the lethargy and depression which tells one that he is far, far from his Father's house, alone, poor, unloved and miserable; that tells another that he is surrounded only with inharmony, that no one understands or loves or appreciates him; that tells another that the struggle homeward is too fierce, that the waves of life in the world are sweeping over him and must carry him out and away; that there is no actual proof of the glory of the Lord. Another says, 'Let me thrust my hands into the nail prints. Let me prove that this Christ whom I have daily crucified still lives. To me words are of no avail. I have outgrown your phrases and am tired of words; tired of hearing the reiteration of those great things which for me never come to pass. Why do they not, if all this is true?'

What holds you back?

"If you have faith as a grain of mustard seed you may say to this mountain, Be ye removed, and it will obey you." What is the mountain? It is the thing that holds you back. It is the condition that stands between you and the realization. It is the crowd that separates you from the Mystic Christ as He passes by. Seek diligently in your hearts and remove it. Follow swiftly and touch His robe, and believe in the healing force that flows from Him for your regeneration."

Why seek the living among the dead?

"Ye who have been called from out the darkness of the ages! Awake today to your great privileges and possibilities! Already out of the darkness of the night, while you slumber and sleep, goes forth the cry, 'Behold! The Bridegroom cometh!' This is no fanciful imagining. It is a reality, a reality of the Soul. Why weep ye? Why seek ye the living among the dead things of the outer life?"

"How often have you gathered together in the past when clouds of darkness, of ignorance, and superstition hung low over humanity, when there could be no hope of immediate surcease from your watching and waiting! How often has each one of you gone boldly forth in past incarnations, giving your lives for that which you believed to be Truth! By such steps and sacrifices have you, little by little, wandered onward and upward until today I find you in this Mystic Order. And still I feel a sadness over the hearts of many that is like a pall of darkness. I hear the cry, 'I cannot, oh, I cannot conquer,' or 'I am so cast down and disappointed. Why tarries my glory so long?' And yet, even while this sad cry lingers in your hearts, even while the teardrops glisten in your lashes, lo! without, upon the mountain top, the sound of eager feet and the shouting of the multitude 'Behold! The Bridegroom cometh! Go ye forth to meet him!'"[14]

The mystic realization.

"How is this going forth to be accomplished? It is the going forth from your mental environment, from that which you have falsely created; the donning of your wedding garment that you may be ready

---

[14] *A Message from the Master*, Curtiss.

to do homage to the coming Bridegroom; the shaking off of the darkness of despair and sorrow that you may join in the glad hymns of welcome as He cometh. Verily, verily, as you enter into this mystic realization, which means so much to your spiritual growth, you will meet the Bridegroom in proportion to the power of the realization you have of the meaning of what you are privileged to receive."[14]

Forget your mistakes.

"All the trials through which you are passing are but the mud of the journey clinging to your feet. Here is your Father's home; the sanctuary of peace and love. Here must you put off your shoes that you may enter cleanly shod. And oh! while you are here, forget the muddy way you have trodden! Realize that here you really touch the outer robe of the glory of the Master. If you can realize this and, like the woman who touched the robe of Jesus in the crowd, believe that virtue has gone forth from the touch, then will the Son of Man turn and look at you and you shall see Him face to face. Only such faith believes that the touch of His garment can heal. In the hurrying crowd this woman, who was poor and old and sick, still had the faith to believe that could she but touch His robe she would be healed. And, lo! it was more than that, for He turned and looked upon her." [14]

Face to face.

"This is the lesson I would leave with you. The Robe of the Mystic Christ is the work He is putting forth; is the love that He is pouring into the hearts that are open to receive it; is the magnetic bond of sympathy that you feel one toward the other; is the responsive love that thrills you as you read these teachings; is the vision of the power of the Mystic Christ within you to conquer, which these teachings awaken in you. This is the Robe, the outer covering of the Mystic Christ. Touch it in faith. Feed on it in your hearts by faith and thanksgiving. Believe in its power. Believe that it is in very truth His garment. Then He will turn and look and you shall see Him face to face."[14]

CHAPTER V

RECOMMENDATIONS FOR DAILY LIFE

WHEN the reader has assimilated the ideas contained in the previous chapters, he will realize that the attainment of union with his Higher Self, which is one with God, is a duty, nay a pleasure, which he owes to himself and to the world. He is then recommended to formulate for himself a plan of acting by which he will eventually attain his ideal. The plan should include *a certain time set aside* for study, for recreation and for *meditation and spiritual realization*, as well as for the activities of the material life.

And this routine, once carefully laid out, should be followed religiously, but with such reasonable latitude that the routine does not become the master instead of the servant; that the follower does not become pedantic, intolerant, or fanatical, instead of becoming a well-balanced, poised, and adaptable Soul. For he who seeks to attain the highest by following one impulse today and another tomorrow, unbalanced by discretion and wisdom; who does one thing today because it appeals to his mood and neglects all other parts of the plan and all other duties cannot expect to advance in a well-balanced manner.

The self-discipline of a definite plan, developed in a certain order and according to a general routine makes for well-balanced and harmonious progress in the spiritual life as well as in the physical. Yet man must always be the master and dictator of his own life, never a slave to his self-appointed and needful rules; for over all these rules is a higher law whose mandates must be observed, i.e., the personal guidance of his Real Self. His daily life should be arranged in such an orderly fashion that he can easily set it aside temporarily at the call of the Real Self, without upsetting it. This he could not do if his life were in confusion.

To listen to the Voice of Intuition and *to be ever responsive to inspiration* is essential to spiritual progress, even if it temporarily interrupts the routine. But there is much to be accomplished between the periods of inspiration, if the new ideas thus received are to be worked out and made to manifest effectively in the life. Inspiration will be more dependable if there be a regular time set apart for its recognition and reception. By following this method the inspiration becomes so frequent as ultimately to be a continuous conscious guidance in all things, both great and small.

The *study* of spiritual things should be carried out at regular times, and special attention should be given to the symbolic or hidden aspects as contrasted with the historical or material viewpoints. If this is done, the Higher Self will be more able to inspire and help to a realization of truth.

Meditation is turning over in the mind a thought or idea that you may see it from every standpoint and grasp all its phases and relations. It is an active mental process, which forms a necessary part of every spiritual student's routine. The first step towards meditation is concentration, the focusing of the attention upon the chosen subject or idea. Then, keeping the mind poised upon the subject, the imagination should be used in thinking out its relation to yourself, to other people, and other parts of the subject. Take a text from the *Bible* such as: "Where two or three are gathered together in My name, there am I in the midst," "I and my Father are One," etc., or some thought such as "Truth," "Purity," "Love," etc., and spend ten minutes in dwelling on its various aspects. This should be a daily pleasure.

Spiritual realization.

The object of spiritual realization is to make real to us that which we know is Truth but which appears to the senses as unreal. Thus, we should endeavour to realize our oneness with God, the action of the Christ-force pouring through all creation, spiritualizing and uplifting it, etc. This endeavour, which is the real object of all religion, is also called Contemplation or Entering the Silence and is usually the culmination of a series of steps in a regular order, thus:

(a) Relaxation.
(b) Concentration.
(c) Meditation.
(d) Realization or Entering the Silence.

When Jesus told his disciples to enter into the closet and shut the door, the closet referred to the Silence, and the "door" which they were to shut was the door of the mind. The Father which seeth in secret is the Higher Self, who does not require words, but who seeth in secret, i.e., in the Silence, through vibrations of love. The open reward is the peace, comfort and spiritual upliftment which comes as the result of such communing with the Father-in-heaven.

To remind ourselves of the God-consciousness within and to aid us in focusing the creative power of our thought upon it, we should avail ourselves of every aid to this end, such as ceremonies, prayers, mantra, set times for devotion and worship, the occurrence of sunrise, noon, and sunset, or any other factor that will help to keep before our mind's eye the ideal to be attained.

Special concentration hours.

We request that all pupils who earnestly desire to co-operate in this Movement or who have the success of this Order at heart, pause for a moment *each* day as near the stroke of noon as possible and send a prayer or a vital creative thought of love to this Center, that it may be perfected in purity and power to accomplish its great mission for humanity. This should not interfere with your daily activities, for you have only to turn mentally to this Center and say, "In the name of the Living Christ may the Heart Center of *The Order of Christian Mystics* be preserved as a pure channel through which Divine Love, Life, and Wisdom may manifest. May increasing power be given it to accomplish its great work for humanity."

When repeating this prayer, realize that the Heart Center includes more than those personalities at the Center who are engaged in the work of the Order, for the Heart Center of every movement includes the heart-love of all members, no matter where they may be. Hence your loving thoughts directed towards helping the Order will form a magic chain uniting all true members in the bonds of love. It will also create a vortex into which there will irresistibly be drawn the positive force of the Divine.

Do not try to make the time coincide with the same hour in Washington. Take the time of your own locality. For, as it is noon somewhere all the time, and as we have pupils in all parts of the world, the repetition of this prayer at noon will make a continuous stream of force pouring into the Center unceasingly.

To come into close vital touch with this Order, each pupil should set apart at least fifteen minutes (thirty if possible) every Sunday evening between 8:00 and 8:30, during which the effort should be made to correlate with the special meeting held at the Center at that time.

At that time each should repeat, either aloud or mentally, the Prayer of Devotion and the Healing Prayer, and concentrate on coming to this Center in thought, realizing that at this time the Master is in the midst of His children; that His love includes all, no matter how distant; that at this time especially He is gathering all together to bless them, and that the streams of love and healing power are going out over the lines of force which connect each pupil with this Center. Over these lines of force the pupils on their part should send their love and help and a strong will that this Movement shall lack for nothing (either spiritually or materially) to make it a powerful factor on all planes to help humanity.

While the helpful forces are sent out

to all alike, nevertheless those who thus consciously correlate with them and who give of their substance—which includes their love and earnest desire to help on all planes—will receive in exact proportion to the earnestness and devotion they express, for, by their desire to become co-workers in this Movement for the upliftment of humanity, they are literally merging themselves into oneness with the streams of living force poured out by the Lodge through this Order; for their desires are creative and will bring forth after their kind.

If any find it impossible to be alone at this time, let them at least send us a strong thought of loving help, even if they are in the midst of a crowd.

The Founders will be glad to know of any experiences the pupils may have in correlating with the Center in this service.

APPENDIX

Part I

ANNOUNCEMENT

"Behold, I bring you good tidings of great Joy."

To ALL earnest seekers after spiritual truth whose sincere desire is to progress in the spiritual life, and who wish the opportunity of coming into closer touch with those Masters of Wisdom who, through all ages, have been the Teachers, Guides and Elder Brothers of humanity, there comes the following message:

In accordance with the geometrical design of the universe, a point in evolution has now been reached when an advanced Order has been established upon the earth-plane to give once more a universal conception of Truth, but couched in modern terms and including, instead of excluding, the many advances in science, invention, historical research, etc., of the twentieth century.

This Order is not an organization in the general acceptance of the term. Its founders and agents are not pupils of any human teacher or "astral guide," nor is the Order *connected with either the outer or inner work of any occult organization now in existence on the physical-plane*, yet it aims to include the best in all similar movements.

The fellowship of The Order of Christian Mystics.

The Order of Christian Mystics is but one name for a great Cosmic Order which has always existed and through which all Souls who have reached Mastery have passed on some plane, at a certain stage of their evolution. It has been represented upon the earth-plane at certain cyclic intervals in all ages, and been known under various names, yet always emphasizing the universality of Truth and presenting a Cosmic Philosophy which can be interpreted and used by every sincere seeker after Truth from his own angle of vision, and at any stage of unfoldment he may reach.

Its manifestation upon the earth-plane during the present cycle began on January 1st, 1908, its numerical name, *The Order of the 15*, being then used. But now that the Order is reaching that great class who are looked upon as orthodox Christians, yet who are eagerly seeking more definite instruction concerning the mysteries of the spiritual life, the name of the philosophy which the Order presents is used instead.

The Order of Christian Mystics is a non-sectarian, unifying spiritual movement, inspired by an unselfish love for humanity and a desire to help mankind recognize the reality of and make practical use of its spiritual guidance in the daily life.

It is Christian in that it seeks the universal Cosmic Christ Principle, no matter by what name that Universal Principle is known in other lands; and in that it bases its teachings on the Christian rather than on Oriental scriptures. It is Mystic in that it teaches its pupils the mystery of how to come into personal and conscious touch with the Christ-consciousness within, and with the Spiritual Teachers in the higher realms.

It is not put forth to form a new sect or cult or further to divide up and separate humanity, or to form another pigeonhole in which to isolate a few followers; nor does it seek to secure a following for any human leader or personality.

It affords a haven of rest for the many weary, storm-tossed souls who have met with disappointment after disappointment in following, one after the other, the great claims made by the popular cult of the moment, for at present the great mass of seekers still run after every forceful personality. The students of this Order are taught to follow impersonal principles, laws and spiritual truths, not personalities.

It comforts and encourages those who are discouraged by the many man-made limitations which seem to hedge about the approach to the realization of the Inner Life or to the personal contact with the higher Spiritual Teachers of mankind; those who have knocked at so many gates and sought in so many avenues only to find that unless they believe as they are told and accept Truth as interpreted by a particular cult and accept blindly the word of those mortals who stand at a particular gate, they cannot hope to enter into a realization of the Divine within themselves or hope for recognition by the Great Ones.

To all such the *Fellowship of the Order of Christian Mystics* brings a message of Freedom, Light, and Satisfaction; Freedom through the Light of Knowledge of spiritual laws and a realization of the graciousness of God to *all mankind*.

"And ye shall know the Truth, and the Truth shall make you free." The knowledge and realization of the Truth is *unto all people*. There is no exclusiveness or favoritism in Truth. All is open *to those who qualify*, not by outer ceremonies, but by preparing themselves within to correlate with the higher phases of consciousness and realization.

Since all men have their own way of looking at Truth and can accept and realize it best along that line, the Great Teachers of humanity have established the *Order of Christian Mystics* as a great clearing house for all phases of Truth, without the limitations of creed and dogma; an Order in which an all-inclusive philosophy can be expounded and the fundamental laws of manifestation underlying all phases of life, consciousness, and evolution can be presented impersonally to all, no matter what their race, color, religion, or stage of unfoldment.

Therefore the *Order of Christian Mystics* is a spiritual Movement, without creed, dogma, rules, or pledges. Instead of emphasizing the differences between its teachings and all others, it strives to establish a platform so universal that its pupils can find in it some one thing to which they can agree, even though that one thing be not the same for all. Thus this Order, therefore, should become a link to join the best efforts of all into one great universal movement which shall spread Brotherhood upon the Earth through spiritual understanding.

True Brotherhood does not mean that all must think alike, but that each recognize Truth wherever found and *demonstrate* love and tolerance toward those who find a different aspect of Truth more helpful.

This Order does not ask its pupils to leave any church, society, or organization to which they feel attracted, unless they find in this Order their true spiritual home and desire to work exclusively with it. It but seeks to help all to understand the workings of the great fundamental Laws of Life, and thus enable them to do their own work the better, in their own way and place.

It asks no one to subordinate his individuality or to follow any leader, but leaves all free to follow the Truth as revealed to them. It does not require that any of its teachings be accepted by its students because some authority says they are true, for unless a teaching appeals to the heart and rings true to a Soul it is not true to the consciousness of that Soul. Hence, *no authority is enforced*, except the authority of that Voice within each heart which recognizes and witnesses to Truth wherever found.

Understand this point clearly: It will be *only through your own individual effort*, your attitude of Soul, and the character of your subsequent life that will enable *you to place yourself* in personal, conscious touch with the Masters of Wisdom. *It depends upon no personality but your own.*

Organizations.

All organizations and movements which receive help from the spiritual-plane have their own particular work to do. Whether they have succeeded in the task set before them, or whether they have failed, is clearly shown by their results, and the same rule must be applied to the work of this Order. But many students have outgrown organizations, having found them too narrow and their necessary limitations too binding. Hence, in this Order an avenue of instruction and help has been put forth that *is not an organization* and which is not limited in its activities.

This Movement is not an organization, because it has no constitution or by-laws, no officers (except the Founders), requires no pledges and no dues, and does not restrict a student's activity in any society or organization. Therefore it is *not antagonistic to, nor a rival of*, any existing organization that is helping humanity, but permits perfect freedom. It holds out the hand of Brotherhood to each and gives all an opportunity to *prove* their ideals of Brotherhood and tolerance which they profess.

As to other movements.

We can but reiterate that while *The Order of Christian Mystics* stands alone, nevertheless it stands for Truth wherever found, its motto being, "By their fruits ye shall know them."

Under no circumstances does it criticize any. If an organization, society, or movement has helped one Soul to take one step upon the Path to Mastery, it has not wrought in vain.

"Whosoever shall give to drink unto one of these little ones a cup of cold water only in the name of a disciple, verily I say unto you, he shall in no wise lose his reward!. . . . Inasmuch as ye have done it unto one of the least of these, my brethren, ye have done it unto me."

The fact that a movement no longer appeals to you, no matter how helpful it may be to others, is evidence either that your Soul has learned the lessons that movement had for you—even though not mastered intellectually—or that it is not your true spiritual home. Hence, to remain connected with an organization to which you no longer feel drawn or which you have outgrown is as detrimental to your Soul-growth as it would be for a flower to remain in a pot which had become too small for it or whose soil had become exhausted.

Each movement that aims to help humanity has its own place and its own work. Colored blocks are necessary in the kindergarten, primers for children, text-books for the training of the mind in school and college. But when the mind has been trained it must then put that training to use in a practical way; in business, under the head of the firm or manager; in art, under a great teacher; in spiritual things, under a Master of Wisdom. In advanced teachings each Soul must use all its experience, discrimination, and intuition to discover which movement really teaches best how to apply spiritual principles to the development within on the Path to Mastery while still meeting the conditions of daily life.

But remember that, because you are no longer interested in the colored blocks or primers you once thought so beautiful, you are not to despise the children who still cling to them, nor find fault with the teachers of the a-b-c's. All have their place, and the children will grow away from the blocks when they have learned their lesson, just as you have grown away from earlier conceptions.

The fact that a teaching attracts and helps you is evidence that it contains the lessons needed by you for the step you are taking. It is not a question of how much ancient, mystical lore or rituals or ceremonies you may know or how many "degrees" you have been put through in other organizations, but how you have learned to *demonstrate the principles* back of all these, in recognizing and correcting your faults, and in growing closer in love and understanding to your fellow men. Every sincere and uplifting movement or teaching has its place and has for followers those who need the lessons expressed in its particular way.

One of the chief objects of this Movement is to reach the great mass of people who will not join organizations or occult societies of any kind. Our language will purposely be made simple, and the great truths which we set forth, as to man and his relation to God and the universe, will be so stated as to appeal to minds which have not delved into the mystic formulas, jargons, and ceremonies which were the vehicles of Truth during the Dark Ages, and on this account we may disappoint many merely intellectual seekers.

Our greatest object is to help to prepare the hearts and minds of mankind for *the near advent of the great Spiritual World-Teacher who is soon to appear, the Avatar.* For He must come, not to any one sect or movement or people, but to all nations and peoples and to all classes whose hearts are prepared to receive Him, both the learned and the unlearned. For the good news of His quick coming must be given "unto all people," not merely to a few intellectual thinkers or occultists.

While the teachings of this Order are those of the Wisdom Religion, they are not theosophic or rosicrucian in the sense of being put forth by any of the numerous societies bearing those names, for they deal with the Christian *Bible* quite as much as with Eastern or medieval teachings.

There is a real necessity for the various presentations of Truth as given to the world, for just as the climate, flora and fauna of a country, and the language and customs of its people vary in different parts of the world, so must Truth garb itself in habiliments best suited to the development and modes of thought of the people to whom it is given. There is a deep, occult reason underlying this law, and St. Paul recognized it when he said, "Be ye all things unto men."

In the development of all students a point is reached where they need the advanced, *personal* instruction, not of any leaders—*who are themselves but students*—but of One who has at His command all knowledge and all wisdom—i.e., a Master of Wisdom,[1] or of those who prove by their teachings that they are in personal touch with such a Master and are helping in the mighty task of preparing the world for the coming of the Avatar. Such teachers need make no claims for themselves, for their teachings are sufficient evidence. It is in answer to this personal need that the Lodge of Masters has put forth *The Order of Christian Mystics* at this time. It comes as a direct response to the prayers of many, many hearts for more light, love, sympathy, and *personal guidance*.

As this continent will become the home of a new Race which will ultimately perfect itself by the survival and interblending of the fittest of all the races now existing, so must its religious

---

[1] It is understood, of course, that the Founders do not answer the letters or compose the Teachings, except under inspiration. They are merely Agents of the Holy Ones back of the Order, and do not pretend to be the Teacher of the Order. The Teachings themselves are evidence of their sources of Inspiration, Love, and Wisdom.

thought be blended and purified that it may emerge as a pure ray which has gathered unto itself the constructive forces from all its sub-rays without condemning any.

The Order of Christian Mystics is put forth in an effort to awaken the Christ-love in the hearts of men, rather than to cater to the intellect or the desire for psychic powers, for only those who can correlate with the Christ-power can be gathered together to form a nucleus in which this Power can be individualized on Earth. The aim of this Movement is especially to help all peoples to find the deep, underlying, vital truths common to all religions in their own, and differentiate between those vital truths and mere human interpretations, be they ever so ancient or mystical, and thus truly, and in the only way possible, prepare for a Universal Brotherhood on Earth in which each Soul shall find the same vital truths spoken in his own language,[2] i. e.,

---

[2] See *Acts*, II, 6.

couched and taught in terms of the religion in which he was born.

Special objects of the Order.

1. Complete individuality through union with the Higher Self.

The ideal of this Order is one of constant *self-mastery*, in obedience to the personal guidance *from within* and prompted by the ability to help humanity to a greater realization of the Christ consciousness. This is the acme of individualism—Mastery—for the Soul and the acme of oneness for the Race. Necessarily the fundamental assumption is the possibility of each Soul coming into conscious touch with his personal Father-in-heaven.

2. Personal training in the philosophy of life.

The personal training is carried on partly on the inner planes and partly by correspondence with the Teacher of the Order through the Founders. Such correspondence is open to all who need personal help with the problems of their

Soul-life. For adequate reply, the letters should contain not more than three questions. The answers will contain clear explanations of the laws of life which apply to the individual needs of the pupil. Such correspondence is sacredly confidential.

3. A higher standard of purity on all planes.

Ere the pupil can attain to the higher stages of spiritual consciousness he must learn to control his thoughts as well as his words and acts. The highest ideals as to the sacredness and purity of the marriage relation and the creative forces are inculcated.

4. Esoteric interpretation of the Bible.

The special object of these teachings is to bring to the attention of the world, as simply as possible, the Pearls of Wisdom in the teachings of the Master Jesus—pearls that have been overlaid with wordy misconceptions and dogmas so long as to be almost unrecognizable.

Although the Christian *Bible* is one of the greatest occult books ever given to humanity—for it contains not only the wisdom of all prior scriptures, but also a prophecy of the future—yet it is the least understood of any scripture because heretofore all efforts to explain it have been upon a literal, intellectual, material or historical basis and not from the standpoint of its *spiritual symbology* and *esoteric* meaning.

This Order gives its students the esoteric key which enables them to apply the underlying laws of every parable, allegory and miracle to their own spiritual growth.

5. *Training the senses to respond to vibrations from all planes.*

The great psychic awakening now sweeping the world has brought many students to the point where their inner faculties are unfolding. This is a point of great danger, for here the two paths—the Right Hand and the Left Hand—diverge.

This Order offers no formulas or general exercises for developing psychic powers, but teaches that all such faculties should evolve gradually *as a natural result* of normal spiritual growth. To seek them in the séance room or to force them through special forms of concentration or negative "sitting for development," etc., is abnormal. But, as the Soul evolves, the senses must respond to higher notes of vibration and awaken to higher states of consciousness. *When this occurs* the pupil must be taught both how to protect himself from the many dangers of the psychic realm[3] and also how to make the best use of the newly acquired powers in furthering his spiritual growth; for psychic powers in themselves *are not an evidence of spirituality*, merely evidence that the student is opening his five senses to the ethereal or astral world, and all depends upon the use he makes of the powers attained. This is a personal work which could not be accomplished by any organization bound by set rules.

6. *Preparation for the Coming World Teacher, The Avatar.*

---

[3] See *Realms of The Living Dead*, Curtiss.

Like nearly all advanced thinkers and movements along spiritual lines, this Order expects a great spiritual Teacher to appear on Earth during the early years of this century. The prophecy, "Many shall come in my name, saying, I am Christ; and shall deceive many," is being literally fulfilled today. This Order fully explains the true mysticism and fundamental laws of the Coming that the Elect may not be deceived.[4] For just as lightning flashes from heaven as the result of the gathering on Earth of certain forces which induce its descent, so must the Coming be the result of the gathering of the forces of love, tolerance, and brotherhood which shall induce its physical manifestation. Hence one of the great objects of this Order is so to train its pupils that, *through their own intuitions*, they may learn to recognize and respond to the influence of that Great Teacher upon the higher planes

---

[4] This is fully explained in *The Voice of Isis*, Curtiss, Chapter X, and especially in *The Message of Aquaria*, Curtiss.

and not be led astray by personality. For one who requires to be told by another, "Lo! here, Lo! there," cannot recognize the manifestation when it takes place.

7. *Special training in recognizing the oneness of Truth wherever found.*

Since the human race reflects Truth, as a diamond reflects light, through many facets, Universal Brotherhood can never be achieved by all men thinking alike. Our idea of Brotherhood is universal recognition of the oneness of Truth in its various expressions or unity in diversity, thereby manifesting perfect tolerance toward all. But we must remain firmly grounded in that aspect of Truth which we have chosen *because we have proved that it is the best for us.*

Financial obligations.

In a Movement such as this the financial side must be fully understood. Although spiritual teachings must be given freely "without money and without price" to all who ask, yet in the present world conditions the help thus asked cannot be presented to the world without the financial co-operation of all who receive and desire to see that help extended more widely. The Founders of the Order give all their time and talents without salary, although, of course, they must be adequately supported if they are to be free to devote their undivided attention to the work of the Order. But if the Teachings are to be issued regularly and the personal letters answered promptly, salaries must be paid to obtain trained and competent workers to perform the great amount of clerical and office work, pay for printing, advertising, etc., connected with such a worldwide Movement.

In the past the work and growth of the Order has been greatly hampered and the personal letters delayed by the lack of adequate assistance in the office work, the Founders having had to use up their valuable time and energy folding lessons, filing letters, etc., when they should have nothing to do but transcribe the inspiration and teachings so freely given them, and reply to the many cries for love, enlightenment, and help from all parts of the world. But as we enter the New Era now opening before the Order and see the tremendous amount of work which should be accomplished in the garnering of the harvest, we must impress upon the minds of all who receive the great spiritual benefits and the practical, personal help from the Order, that a *mighty opportunity* is placed before them *through this Order* to co-operate for the enlightenment and uplift of humanity.

But to accomplish this the Founders must be freed from all the mechanical details and be enabled to devote their entire time to writing and teaching. Therefore, financial support *sufficient to accomplish this is* an obligation which every student should gladly assume. If the teachings help you it will be evidence that *they can help other*s, hence that you can best serve humanity by making it possible to spread *these particular teachings* abroad.

The Law of Justice permits humanity to be helped only to the extent that, through its own efforts, it makes it possible for the help to reach it. If you feel an inner urge to study with us, and if you find that the lessons help you, you will naturally desire to make it possible for other Souls to receive the same. Therefore, out of pure love *and a desire to help others* you will give as much as you can afford. Let all give *according to their ability*.

A simple announcement of your desire to study with us *and a realization of your obligation to help us in return* is all that is necessary. The help we ask is just what your conscience tells you is the right and proper thing to do *in accordance with your worldly means*. In short, it must be looked upon *as a privilege to co-operate* in this great work.

All contributions, both large and small, will be gratefully received and promptly acknowledged. No matter what amount is given, the real offering is the loving desire to help. "Let every man do according as he is disposed in his heart, not grudgingly, or of necessity, for God loveth a cheerful giver."

You will greatly facilitate our work if before asking questions in regard to it you will carefully study this pamphlet to see if the information you desire is not contained therein.

Our correspondence is so large that we cannot answer letters immediately, but will always endeavor to do so as soon as possible after their receipt.

For lessons of the O. C. M. address
F. HOMER CURTISS, M. D.
3510 Quebec St., N. W.
Washington, D. C.

APPENDIX

Part II

The object of study classes.

As we have said elsewhere, "The object of all religions is worship of the Divine. And the primary object of all worship is personal contact with and realization of the Divine. But as there is a method or mechanism by which the whole manifested universe comes into physical expression, so is there a method or mechanism by which conscious contact is made between the human personality and those higher expressions of God toward which the heart aspires." Therefore, the primary object of the Teachings of this Order is not mere intellectual information, but conscious contact with the Divine and the development of intuition and inner spiritual guidance. These are heart qualities and powers which require spiritual and devotional exercises for their development. Hence the devotional exercises with which the meetings should be opened and closed are more important than the intellectual discussion. For while a clear understanding of our cosmic philosophy will enlighten the mind, expand the consciousness, and give a greater understanding of life, only prayer, aspiration, and devotion will unfold and manifest our spiritual nature, the great object for which we incarnated here on Earth.

How to form a study class.

In the study of mysticism and occultism, in addition to the careful reading and meditation upon the ideals presented, it is helpful to have a number who are interested in the same teachings organize a class and study together. The union of the auras of a number of harmonized students who are sincerely aspiring for a greater realization of light, life, and love creates a vortex of spiritual force into which the return currents of enlightenment on the subject studied and of life and love are naturally drawn.

Arrange to meet regularly at some convenient place such as a member's home, in the evening if possible, as this permits both men and women to attend, and choose one of your members to read the lesson. Select a few pages of the book a week in advance of the meeting, and have each member carefully study and meditate upon them during the week, making notes of the ideas that seem most important

Begin promptly at the hour designated. Open the meeting with the hymns indicated, followed by a period of Silence in which you still your mind, turn the current of your thoughts from the affairs of daily life, and concentrate them upon the Prayer for Light or some harmonizing topic announced beforehand such as harmony, peace, light, love, understanding, etc.

After the class has been harmonized by the hymns and blessed by the prayer and meditation, have the leader read a few lines from the lesson selected and all who feel so prompted comment thereon, especially giving the new ideas that may have come to them during their study. Invite interruptions and discussion. Any questions which cannot be answered by the discussion may be referred to some member or members to look up in the index of "The Curtiss Books" and report at the next meeting. If not settled thus, the questions should be referred to the Superintendent of Local Centers, who will submit them to the Teacher and explanations will be returned as soon as possible.

Keep a kindly but firm rein over all discussions, allowing plenty of latitude, so long as it does not stray too far away from the subject. *Studiously avoid arguments.* One should state one's interpretation of the passage under discussion and let it rest there.

Especially do not bring in the teachings of other schools or authors, no matter how excellent they may be. To do so would bring in thought currents from other sources than this Order's and so tend to cause confusion and argument. The class meets primarily to find out what *this Order* teaches, hence the time should be given exclusively to its teachings. It will be excellent training in clear thinking to formulate your opinion as definitely as possible. Do not try to convince others or impose your views upon them. Simply state your views and grant to others the same freedom of thought and expression which you desire for yourself.

Above all be cheerful and good natured and *let peace, harmony and love abound*, for without these conditions the study will degenerate into mere intellectual discussions and the Voice of Intuition which you are seeking to cultivate will be drowned out.

In this way the meetings become intensely interesting, intellectually stimulating and enlightening, and spiritually helpful, for the different viewpoints brought out serve to make clear phases of the subject not always expressed in the printed lesson. Thus discussed, one lesson will often extend over two or three meetings.

Strive ever to bring out the heart or Christ-conception in all your discussions of the lesson, not permitting the intellectual to predominate. Seek for the loving help that is contained in each lesson and always conclude by pointing it out plainly so that all can see and carry it home with them.

Let all the students strive continually to spread the Teachings wherever and whenever Wisdom inspires you, but do not seek to force them upon anyone. Invite your friends to the meetings, those you are led to talk to and who become interested, but do not be anxious about their coming, leaving all free to follow the leadings of their own hearts.

Send in monthly or quarterly reports of the progress of your meetings and of different members, always encouraging, however, personal correspondence direct with the Order when a student is confronted with a vital Soul problem.

If a name is chosen for the class, remember that names have occult powers and the class will have to demonstrate that it can live up to the name chosen.

After the class has been working harmoniously for some time, if it is desired to expand into a Local Center of the Order to carry on a more organized line of work, write for further information.

ORDER OF SERVICE

1. Hymn. Selected.
2. Hymn of Consecration. (Music, Unity Hymn 46)
3. Prayer for Light, with Meditation, and Visualization.
4. Study and Discussion of Lesson.
5. Prayer for World Harmony.
6. Prayer for Demonstration.
7. Healing Song.
8. Healing Prayer.
9. Mention of the Heart Center and the Founders, also the names of Individuals whom you wish helped.
10. Closing Verse.

APPENDIX
PART III

Prayers of The Order of Christian Mystics.[1]

PRAYER FOR LIGHT
O Christ! Light Thou within my heart
The Flame of Divine Love and
   Wisdom,
That I may dwell forever in the radiance of Thy countenance
And rest in the Light of Thy smile!

PRAYER FOR WORLD HARMONY
Glory and honor and worship be unto
   Thee, O Lord Christ,
Thou who art the Life and Light of all
   mankind.
Thou art the King of Glory to whom
   all the peoples of the Earth should
   give joyful allegiance and service.

---

[1] For others see *Prayers of the O. C. M.*, Curtiss.

Inspire mankind with a realization of true Brotherhood.
Teach us the wisdom of peace, harmony and co-operation.
Breathe into our hearts the understanding that only as we see ourselves as parts of the one body of humanity can peace, harmony, success and plenty descend upon us.
Help us to conquer all manifestations of inharmony and evil in ourselves and in the world.
May all persons and classes and nations cease their conflicts, and unselfishly strive for peace and good-will.
Bless us all with the radiance of Thy Divine Love and
Wisdom that we may ever worship Thee in the beauty of holiness.
In the Name of the Living Christ we ask it. Amen.

PRAYER OF DEMONSTRATION
I am a child of the Living God!
I have within me the all-creating power of the Christ!

It radiates from me and blesses all I contact.
It is my Health, my Strength, my Courage,
My Patience, my Peace, my Poise,
My Power, my Wisdom, my Understanding,
My Joy, my Inspiration, and my Abundant Supply.
Unto this great Power I entrust all my problems,
Knowing they will be solved in Love and Justice.
(Mention all problems connected with your worldly affairs, visualize each and conclude with the following words)
O Lord Christ! I have laid upon Thy altar all my wants and desires.
I know Thy Love, Thy Wisdom, Thy Power and Thy Graciousness.
In Thee I peacefully rest, knowing that all is well.
For Thy will is my will. Amen.

HEALING PRAYER
    O thou loving and helpful Master
        Jesus!
    Thou who gavest to Thy disciples
        power to heal the sick!
    We, recognizing Thee, and realizing
        Thy divine Presence with us,
    Ask Thee to lay Thy hands (powers)
        upon us in healing Love.
    Cleanse US from all OUR sins, and
        by the divine power of Omnipotent
        Life,
    Drive out the atoms of inharmony and
        disease, and
    Fill our bodies full to overflowing
        with Life and Love and Purity.

HYMN OF CONSECRATION — MUSIC
    Within each heart a sacred Flame,
        The Christ Star's steady blaze;
    Help us Thy children, gracious Lord,
        On it to fix our gaze.

    A holy sanctuary there
        Far from the world's mad din.
    Grant us Thy power, O blessed Christ,
        To boldly enter in.

Upon Thy altar lay our hearts,
    Thy covenant is sealed.
We see Thy face, we touch Thy robe,
    And lo! our hearts are healed.

Grant us Thy grace to carry hence
    To all the world this Love,
To help to lead Thy children, Lord,
    Into Thy courts above.

Harriette Augusta Curtiss.

HEALING SONG — MUSIC
Blessed Savior, assist us
    To rest on Thy word.
Let Thy soul-healing Power
    On us now be outpoured.
Wash away every sin-spot;
    Take perfect control;
Say to each trusting spirit,
    "Thy faith makes thee whole."

Chorus

Wilt thou be made whole?
Wilt thou be made whole?
Oh, come weary suff'rer,
Oh, come sin-sick soul!

See, the life-stream is flowing!
See, the cleansing waves roll!
Step into the current
And thou shalt be whole. Amen.

HEALING VERSE
Watch by the sick,
Enrich the poor
With blessings from
Thy boundless store.
Be every mourner's sleep tonight
Like infants' slumber pure and bright.
Amen.

INDEX

Angels, Arch, 14, 32; Hymn about, 33
Anger, 44
Appendix, 101, 127, 134
Asceticism, 40
Authority, the only, 108
Avatar, The, 73, 81, 113, 120

Baptist, John the, 62
Bee, 28
Blood, mystic, 80-4
Body, training of, 39, 40-1
Bread, Living, 80
Bridegroom, 87-9
Brotherhood, true, 107

Christ-consciousness, 19, 60, 79
Christ, center, 75; story, 54-5; historic, 68, 70; Mystic, 66, 73-8, 85
Control, of self, 60
Co-operation, the Law, 24-5
Correlate, choose to, 13, 14
Criticize, 65; never, 110
Cymbals, 85

Desires, natural, 39
Discipleship, path of, 34, 49
Discipline, needed, 40-1, 93

Index

Diver, simile of, 38

Evil, resist not, 45
Evolution begins, 10
Express, now, 6, 7

Face of the Silence, 18
Faith, of woman, 89
Feet, dancing, 85
Flesh, mystical, 80-1
Flowers, don't say it with, 7

Gland, pineal, 75
Guidance, 41

Happiness, 5, 7, 8, 50
Heart, center, 75; doctrine, 14
Heathen, the only, 18

Help, super-human, 48

Ideal, highest worthy, 3
Illumination, 52
Indweller, Prayer to, 46
Inspiration, 74
Intellect, 60-1
Intuition, 67, 94

Jesus, Avatar, 73, 81; flesh of, 80

Krishna, Rama, 17

Life, family, 3; in higher realms, 4; mental, 3; outer, public, 3; psychic, 3; real or Souls, 4; to live, 7
Lives, our many, 3

Love, Cosmic, Divine, 20

Meditation, daily, 65, 94-7
Mist, mental, 2
Mortals, as avenues, 13; man not a, 37, 43
Mystery, all life a, 1
Mystic, not a dreamer, 2

Nationalism, 22
Necessity, Cycle of, 11
Noon, prayer service, 97
NRA, 25

Order, a cosmic, 102; object of, 116-7

Paul, doctrine of, 70-2-6

Pineal, gland, 75
Plexus, solar, 75
Prayer, noon, 97; of the Order, 134
Production, mass, 26

Reaction, causes suffering, 43
Realization, 95
Recapitulation, 64
Recommendations, 93
Religion, a path, 16-7
Resurrection, 32-3
Robe, touched, 89

Sacrifice, Law of, 8,9
Sadhana, 18
Satisfaction, 4, 5, 6
Service, order of, 133

Sheep, other, 19
Silence, entering, 96
Solar plexus, 75
Study-class, 127-8
Suffering, causes of, 43
Sun, function of, 74;
  Spiritual, 15, 81

Surrender, complete, 13

Teachings, Inner, 59
Training, Western, 40

www.ingramcontent.com/pod-product-compliance
Lightning Source LLC
Chambersburg PA
CBHW071506040426
42444CB00008B/1521